Wildflowers

The Pacific Coast

Acknowledgements

As is true of any project, this book was not done in a vacuum. Many people offered help and encouragement along the way. Because of them, the book was an enjoyable endeavor.

Many people, too numerous to specifically name, were of invaluable assistance in finding good places to photograph wildflowers in Olympic National Park, the Oregon Dunes National Recreation Area, Redwoods National Park, and Prairie Creek Redwoods State Park. I am especially grateful to Dr. Kenton Chambers, Oregon State University, and Dr. John Sawyer, Humbolt State University, for assisting with plant identification and locations and for letting me use the Herbarium facilities of their respective universities. This was especially helpful. Dr. Sawyer also assisted in reviewing the manuscript and made many helpful suggestions that aided its readability.

My husband, Kirk, was both encouraging and helpful, aiding in the selection of photos, proof-reading, and doing many other tedious tasks.

To all these people, I am grateful.

Beth Horn

Wildflowers
The Pacific Coast

A Guide to Selected Wildflowers and Flowering Shrubs
from British Columbia to northern California

by
Elizabeth L. Horn

First Printing July, 1980
Published by Beautiful America Publishing Company
P.O. Box 608, Beaverton, Oregon 97075
Robert D. Shangle, Publisher

This book is dedicated to Francis Horn, who shared his Oregon heritage with me, and to Frances Horn, the granddaughter he never knew, but who now shares in this heritage.

Library of Congress Cataloging in Publication Data
Pacific Coast Wildflowers
1. Wild flowers — Northwest coast of North America — Identification.
2. Coastal flora — Northwest coast of North America — Identification.
I. Title
QK143.H66   582.13′0979   80-15350
ISBN 0-89802-099-9

Contents

Foreword

The Pacific Coast shoreline has an attraction all its own: wind-swept bluffs, damp salt spray, open expanses of golden sand, and vistas of rugged vertical cliffs, all with a background of deep blue ocean or fog-shrouded sea. The northern Pacific Coast is all of these. Wildflowers and flowering shrubs are a part of these scenes and add to their color and appeal.

This book was designed to help you identify the most conspicuous wildflowers and flowering shrubs you will normally encounter in your travels along the Pacific shore from British Columbia to northern California. Over 125 species are portrayed in full color. In addition to the common and scientific name for each plant, I've tried to include information on its range, the kinds of environments where it is found, and its historical uses. This information always makes a plant more interesting and easier to remember. The flowering time and size of many species are also noted. However, these should only be used as general guidelines. Since many of these plants range the full length of the Pacific Coast, they obviously bloom earlier along the California shore than they would along the British Columbia coast. Variations in soil and topography also influence the blooming time as well as the size a plant may grow. The common yarrow, for instance, may grow only a few inches tall on a sandy dune where drying winds blow constantly; on the northern slope of a coastal headland, protected from the wind and firmly rooted in deeper soil, the same species may grow nearly two feet tall!

So take this little book with you when you visit the coast. Use it as an introduction to the many wildflowers you will see. Take the time to learn a little about each as you go. Take note of the type of area where it grows. And consider it a re-found friend when you next encounter it. You'll find that knowing a little about the plants you discover will add a lot of fun to your trip, and make it far more interesting.

Happy flower hunting!

The Coastal Scene

Rugged headlands, small sandy coves, and broad plains that may be partially filled with sand dunes or covered by dense forest blend to produce unmatched scenic variety and beauty. The mild climate facilitates visitation year around and also contributes to the long flowering season. Several interesting shrubs, for instance the chapparral broom and silk tassel, bloom during the winter months. Springtime begins in February and sandy spits and plains may still be covered with blossoms in August.

Our northern Pacific coast is blessed with a moderate climate year around. The constant temperature of the vast Pacific Ocean is largely responsible for this. In addition, northwesterly winds dominate during the summer months (bringing cool air) while southwesterly winds are more prevalent during the winter (bringing warm air). Cool summers and mild winters result. Coastal beaches may be bathed in fog during the summer, especially if a warm air mass sits inland. Coastal precipitation is quite high, especially in the northern part of our range and occurs mostly in the winter. Low temperatures and the presence of fog, however, prevent a real moisture deficit during the summer.

Coastal Vegetation

Climate largely determines the type of vegetation to be found in a given area. However, other conditions are also important. Topography and underlying soils, for example, are very influential. Associations of plants growing together under the same conditions are called plant communities. The collective surroundings of a given plant is its habitat.

The wildflowers and flowering shrubs described in this book are grouped according to the habitats in which they are most typically found. Rarely, however are the lines between these areas completely sharp. Often, one grades into another. For example, where brush has begun to invade an open grassland, salmonberry might be found on the edges of the grassland and be a dominant plant in the resulting brushfield. The tiger lily grows well on exposed, grassy headlands, but also thrives in the partial shade at the edge of a brush thicket. Sometimes conditions may occur to allow a versatile plant to grow successfully in more than one area. Salal, for example, dominates brushy areas along coastal bluffs and forms on almost impenetrable hedge. It also grows as the understory of a shady, coastal forest. Sometimes conditions change with the season. Ladies' tresses, a member of the Orchid Family, is frequently found in moist deflation plains on the lee side of a sand dune. However, by the time it blooms in late July, the sandy substrate may appear quite dry. This seasonal change is also important on many coastal headlands, where a thin layer of soil over the basalt substrate supports a grassy community. Moisture is plentiful in this thin layer of soil during the spring. By mid-summer, the soil is dry.

Nonetheless, most plants typically grow together as a community within a specific type of habitat. You will soon learn that where you find sand verbena, searocket will not be far away. Small creeping buttercup will usually be found not far from golden-eyed grass and tinker's penny. Plants in this book are grouped in five habitats: open beach and dunes, wetlands, cliffs and grasslands, brushfields, and coastal forest.

Open Beach and Dunes.   Few kinds or numbers of plants survive on the open sand of the beach or dunes. The constantly shifting sand provides difficult footing. Most beach adapted plants have deep taproots and stout stems that can adapt to being alternately buried or exposed by the blowing sand. Beach silvertop thrives partly because of its deep taproot. The sheathing petioles or leaf stalks are alternately buried and exposed by the sand. Other plants, such as the sand verbena and beach morning glory have broad, succulent leaves that help trap sand and keep it in place. Most of the plants growing on open sand reproduce vegetatively instead of by seed. Seeds may be buried too deep or left exposed to dry in the salt air and wind. Seeds of the gray beach pea and beach silvertop are exceptions. These seeds are larger and heavier than sand grains allowing them to be buried beneath the sand where they will not dry out. Their weight gives them some stability during the critial germination period. Coast strawberry and Pacific silverweed spread by stolons, much like the garden strawberry does. Horizontal stems spread over the surface and roots form at the nodes, resulting in a new plant.

Wetlands.   Wetlands can be either salt water or fresh. Poor drainage on the flat coastal plain results in many swales and moist roadside ditches. The coast is also dotted with many lakes and marshes. Typical lowland plants of these areas include the cattail, skunk cabbage, spirea, and pond lily. A wetland unique to the coast is the deflation plain where the wind has carried the sand away until the water table is reached. Deflation plains normally occur on the lee side of the foredune, which immediately parallels the shore, or at the base of a large, moving dune system. Typically, some plants of the open beach also occur here. It is rich in plant diversity, consisting mostly of low, herbaceous plants: seashore lupine, ladies' tresses, monkey-flower, gentian, Pacific silverweed, and small creeping buttercup are only a few. A special type of wetland is the coastal bog that forms between coastal dunes or in other places where poor drainage exists. Here several carnivorous plants, the cobra plant and the sundew, are found. They are usually associated with other colorful plants such as the Labrador tea and bog laurel. Unique to the shoreline are saltwater wetlands, where the tide may periodically cover mudflats and bays or fill the mouths of sea-going streams. It is here that you might look for the colorful jaumea and dainty sea milkwort.

Cliffs and Grasslands.   Much of the shoreline is underlain by volcanic headlands of dark basalt. They may be covered with a dense cover of grass on their southern slopes before dropping vertically into the sea. In the spring and early summer, when moisture collects on the surface of the rocks, a myriad of springtime flowers appear. The brightly colored stonecrop nestles in nooks and crannies, its succulent leaves storing moisture during the early summer to be used when the thin soil mantle dries. The columbine, larkspur, footsteps-of-spring, thrift, and tiger lily herald the coming summer. Later, as the slopes begin to dry, a fresh crop of flowers appear—the wild carrot, self-heal, pearly everlasting, daisy, and goldenrod are but a few. These headlands offer spectacular views of the ocean surf, and a wide variety of wildflowers and shrubs. These grassy prairies increase southward along the coast.

Brushfields.   Brushfields are a transition between open grasslands and a forest cover. Shrubs and young trees gradually invade openings, be they grassy meadows, pastures, or partially stabilized dunes. On the coast they are usually very colorful, being made up of some of North America's most spectacular flowering shrubs: the azalea, rhododendron, red-flowering currant, and elderberry. In addition, several exotic species, noticeably gorse and scotch broom, have invaded many coastal areas, often competing with native species. The mild coastal climate encourages luxuriant growth, and often these brushlands are nearly impossible to walk through. They thus have a very important function. They provide a dense cover that protects steep slopes from erosion and provide shelter for various forms of wildlife. The coast of southern Oregon and northern California differ somewhat from that farther north. The shrub and forest communities are replaced by communities of herbs and low shrubs—grass-covered slopes and brushfields dominate. Probably the warmer, drier climate of this stretch of shoreline has much to do with this change. The greater frequency of fog and the predominance of high bluffs and steep slopes immediately adjacent to the ocean may be other factors.

Coastal Forest.   Eventually, trees begin to sprout beneath the brush, grow above the shrubs, and produce a dense canopy that prevents much light from reaching the forest floor. Much of the coastal forest is therefore rather open and park-like. Many of the shrubs of the brushfield persist as part of the understory but they are usually less bushy and have fewer stems. Some wildflowers carpet the forest floor, producing an almost continuous mat—false lily-of-the-valley, miners lettuce, and bleedingheart are good examples. Only five conifer species are prevalent along the coast: shore pine (*Pinus contorta*), sitka spruce (*Picea sitchensis*), Douglas fir (*Pseudotsuga menziesii*), western hemlock (*Tsuga heterophylla*), and along the southern Oregon coast and northern California coast, the coastal redwood (*Sequoia sempevirens*). The shore pine is found just above the high tide line and endures the full effect of wind and salt spray. It can grow in mineral soil and may, when young, form dense thickets in interdunal swales. Sitka spruce is strictly a fog-belt species, and grows only in close proximity to the coast. It can form a dense forest, excluding other species. Because it grows on coastal bluffs, it is often shaped and gnarled by the salt spray and wind. Western hemlock and Douglas fir are not typically shore trees, but are the dominant species of the lowland forests of the Coast Range. Where sand dunes migrate inland, they often bury western hemlock and Douglas fir. The redwood is a unique forest, growing best in a very narrow band along the coast, but less prevalent on ocean-facing slopes because it does not tolerate salt spray.

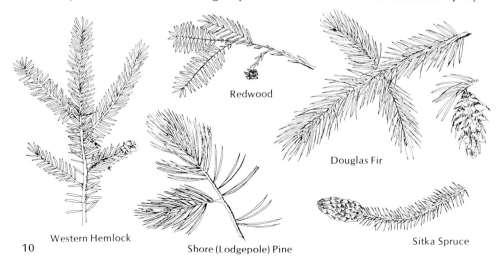

Redwood

Douglas Fir

Western Hemlock

Shore (Lodgepole) Pine

Sitka Spruce

Area Covered: The Pacific Coast

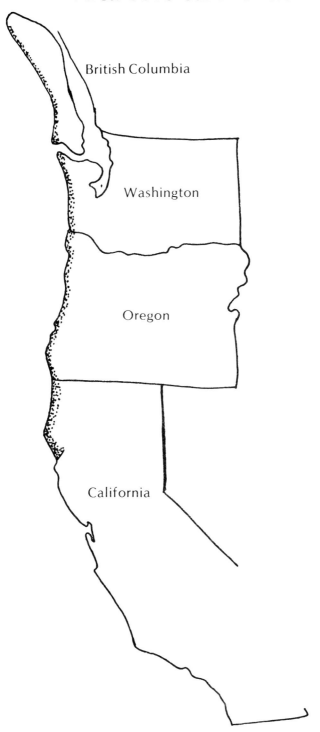

British Columbia

Washington

Oregon

California

How To Use This Book

As you travel along the Pacific Coast, explore its beaches and hike trails to its grassy headlands, you will encounter a rich variety of wildflowers and flowering shrubs. The plants in this book are arranged according to the habitat where they are most often found: beaches and dunes, wetlands, cliffs and grasslands, brushfields, and coastal forest. Look around you and decide which section of the book to look in for your plant. Flowers are arranged by family within these habitat groups so similar plants are together. Match the color photo and simple word description with your plant. Botanical terminology has been kept to a minimum. However, should you encounter a term you do not understand, an illustrated glossary is found.

Each plant heading includes the common name, the scientific name and the family grouping of the plant described. The names are generally taken from Hitchcock and Cronquist (Flora of the Pacific Northwest, University of Washington Press, Seattle 1973).

Selected References

Abrams, Leroy. Illustrated Flora of the Pacific States, Stanford, California, Stanford University Press, 1940, 1950, 1951, 1960, 4 vols.

Ball, Edward K. Early Uses of California Plants, Berkeley, University of California Press, 1972.

Gunther, Erna. Ethnobotany of Western Washington, Seattle, University of Washington Press, 1973.

Hitchcok, C. Leo and Arthur Cronquist. Flora of the Pacific Northwest, Seattle, University of Washington Press, 1973.

Munz, Philip A. and David D. Keck. A California Flora and Supplement, Berkeley, University of California Press, 1973.

Glossary

alternate — usually referring to leaf arrangement, when there is only one at a given place on a stem

annual — a plant that lives only one year

axillary — in the angle between a leaf and stem

basal — at the base

blade — expanded part, for instance the blade of a leaf

bulb — underground cluster of leaves for food storage

biennial — requiring two growing seasons to complete a life cycle

bract — modified or reduced leaf

cleft — cut or divided almost to the middle

compound — divided into more than one part, as opposed to simple (as in leaf)

corm — bulb-like fleshy portion of a stem, usually underground, used for food storage

corolla — inner circle of flower parts (petals)

deciduous — falling off at the end of the growing season

decumbent — lying on the ground near the base, but with the tip elevated

deflation plain — flat, sandy plain where wind has removed sand down to the water table

disk flower — the tubulor flower in members of the Composite Family, e.g. the yellow flowers in the center of a daisy

dissected — deeply cut or divided into many parts

entire — not toothed or cut

evergreen — lasting year around, throughout the year

foredune — first ridge of sand paralleling the beach

gland — organ that secretes material

habitat — place where a plant grows

head — a very compact cluster of flowers

herb — plant without woody parts

lateral — at the side

leaflet — one of the parts of a compound leaf

lip — one of the parts of a two-lipped corolla

lobe — shallow division on a leaf

node — place on a stem that bears a leaf

oblong — leaf form where the length is much greater than the width and the edges are parallel for most of their length.

obovate — leaf form shaped with the narrowest part at the base and the widest at the tip.

opposite — usually referring to leaf arrangement, when two leaves occur directly opposite each other on a stem

ovate — leaf form shaped with the broadest part at the base

palmate — spreading like the fingers of a palm (as compared to pinnate)

panicle — branching flower cluster

pedicel — stalk or stem of a single flower

pendant — hanging

perennial — plant lasting from one year to the next

petal — one of the floral parts, usually colored

petiole — leaf stalk

pinnate — arranged along the side of a central stalk (as compared to palmate)

pistil — central, seed-bearing organ of a plant

prickle — thorn-like projection

prostrate — growing flat on the ground

pubescent — hairy

ray flower — flat, elongate flowers of a composite, e.g. the white marginal flowers of a daisy

raceme — flower cluster where the individual flower pedicels are distributed linearly along a central stalk and the lower flowers open first

rhizome — underground stem

rootstock — underground root-like stem

rosette — collection of leaves arranged circularly around the base of a plant

scorpoid — coiled, curved

sepal — parts of flower below the petal, usually green

sessile — stemless

sheathe — usually when the basal part of a leaf encloses part of the stem

simple — one piece, as opposed to compound (in leaves)

spatulate — narrow at the base and wider at the tip

spur — saclike or tubular projection from a sepal or petal

stamen — floral organ bearing the pollen

sterile — not fertile; will not produce seeds

stigma — pollen-receiving part of the pistil

stolen — a runner or "sucker" that will root to form a new plant

style — stem-like part of the pistil

succulent — fleshy

taproot — main descending root

tendril — slender coiling stem or modified leaf used by a climbing plant to support itself

vegetative — reproducing by means other than seeds

whorl — three or more similar organs radiating from the same spot, e.g. whorled leaves

LEAF ARRANGEMENTS

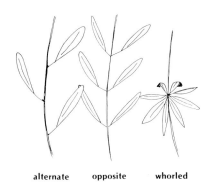

alternate   opposite   whorled

LEAF STRUCTURE

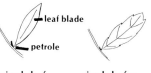

leaf blade

petrole

simple leaf   simple leaf —
pinnately veined

simple leaf —
palmately veined

leaflet

compound leaf —
pinnately compound

compound leaf —
palmately compound

FLOWER PARTS

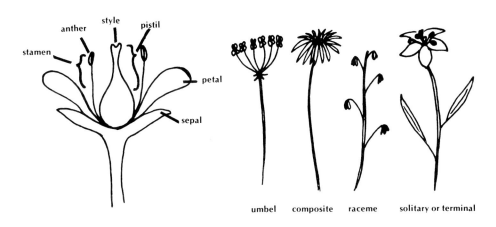

stamen

anther   style   pistil

petal

sepal

TYPES OF FLOWER CLUSTERS

umbel   composite   raceme   solitary or terminal

LEAF SHAPES

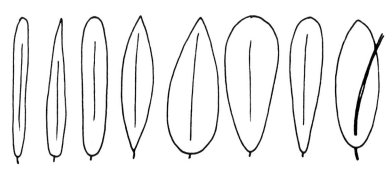

linear   oblong   ovote   spatulate

lanceolate   elliptic   obovate   clasping

Beaches / Dunes

BEACH KNOTWEED   *Polygonum paronychia*   Buckwheat Family

Beach knotweed is a low, sprawling plant with small, green-veined, pale pink flowers in leafy clusters at the tips of the branches. This is a woody plant with inch-long, elliptic leaves. These are rolled under along the edge, a feature that helps conserve moisture along the windy shoreline where this knotweed grows. Beach knotweed is commonly found in dune areas that are undergoing the beginning stages of revegetation and other sandy places along the coast from Vancouver Island to California. It is known as a "pioneer" species because it is able to become established in open dunes as one of the first plants to colonize the sandy substrate.

17

SANDVERBENA   *Abronia latifolia*   Four-O' clock Family

Commonly found covering a mound of sand on open, coastal dunes from Vancouver Island to southern California, yellow sandverbena makes a colorful spot on the sandy landscape. Stout, vertical taproots and the sprawling, branching stems appear to hold the sand and plant in place. The kidney-shaped leaves are glandular, often encased with grains of sand, felt by some to be a further adaptation to life on the unstable sand. The weight of these accumulated sand grains may help hold the plant in place. Although the individual flowers are small, sandverbena is conspicuous because the flowers occur in ball-shaped clusters several inches in diameter. Since sandverbena grows in a loose, sandy substrate that is difficult for seedlings to grow in, much of its reproduction is by vegetative means.

A less common component of our coastal beaches and dunes, pink sandverbena (*Abronia umbellata*) is similar. However, its flowers are slightly smaller and are pink or purple. It occurs from British Columbia to Baja California and is more common along California shores.

The large taproots of the yellow sandverbena were dug and used for food by many coastal Indian tribes. Both the Klallam and the Makah of Washington were known to utilize this food plant, which has been compared to the domestic sugar beet as a food.

18

SEA PURSLANE   *Honkenya peploides*   Pink Family

Also called seabeach sandwort. Sea purslane is not noted for its flowers, which are very tiny, barely an inch across. They are nearly hidden, tucked between the fleshy, inch-long leaves, which appear to wrap around them. This is significant because the species name is derived from the ancient Greek word *peplis*, meaning cloak, and denotes how the leaves wrap around the little green flowers. This plant forms distinctive mounds on many coastal beaches, its somewhat trailing stems sprawling across the beach sand and cobblestones. It is quite cosmopolitan, growing on coastal beaches from Alaska to Oregon and on the Atlantic seacoast of North America, Greenland, Iceland, and northern Asia.

Very few plants are able to tolerate the open beach. Since most seeds are capable of germinating in wet sand, large numbers of seedlings can often be found on the beach in the spring. However, most shortly succumb to the elements. Some do not have the ability to quickly develop an extensive root system to reach deeper water levels as the sand dries at mid-summer. Constant coastal winds may buffet the plant unmercifully before it can establish itself. Salt spray, carried inland by these winds, deposits drying salt particles on the plant's surface. Blowing sand may alternately bury and expose the plant's roots and stem. Very few plants can tolerate this hostile environment. The hardy, bush-like shape and thick cuticle on the leaves and stems contribute to sea purslane's ability to survive on the coastal beach.

SEAROCKET   *Cakile maritima*   Mustard Family

Sprouting on open sand, this little annual has fleshy leaves and stems. Branching freely from the base, some of searocket's stems are upright, others spread across the sand. The alternate leaves are about an inch long and are pinnately lobed. Pale purple flowers are clustered near the ends of the stems. Fairly common on Pacific Coast beaches, searocket blooms through most of the summer. It occurs from British Columbia to California.

One other searocket (*Cakile edentula*) also occurs along our Pacific Coast. The two plants look quite similar; however, the succulent leaves of *Cakile edentula* are merely lobed or wavy-edged, not divided. It occurs from Alaska to California and is also found along the Atlantic and Great Lakes shores.

COAST STRAWBERRY *Fragaria chiloensis* Rose Family

Creeping over sandy bluffs and dry sandy plains, coast strawberry is found from Alaska to California and also grows along the coasts of South America and Hawaii. Coast strawberry has large white, five-petaled flowers that are nearly an inch across and glossy-green, three-parted leaves. It spreads readily by stolons—horizontal stems that grow over the surface of the ground and root to start a new plant. Where coast strawberry is abundant, it nearly spreckles the ground with its white blossoms. The strawberries that appear later in the summer are much smaller than the flowers. Careful searching among the leaves on sandy flats and bluffs should find these tasty, if gritty, morsels. You will have to be early, however, because chipmunks and many species of birds relish these fruits.

Because the shiny leaves and large white flowers are so attractive, coast strawberry is often planted in coastal gardens for a ground cover. Small rooted cuttings do best in sandy, well-drained soil. If placed about 18 inches apart, their stolons will fill in an area in only one growing season. The spot will be particularly attractive if pieces of driftwood are incorporated.

The Rose Family contains some of our most valuable economic plants, largely because of their fruits. Cherries, pears, apples, peaches, plums, and blackberries are only a few examples.

21

PACIFIC SILVERWEED   *Potentilla pacifica*   Rose Family

Pacific silverweed is never far from the coast, preferring sandy bluffs, deflation plains, and wet marsh borders from Alaska to southern California. Like the strawberry, silverweed spreads readily by stolons or runners. Instead of a white flower, however, the silverweed blossom is a bright yellow and is therefore sometimes mistaken for a buttercup. An inch or more across, it is a conspicuous flower. The leaves are pinnately compound, meaning the leaflets are spread linearly along a center line, like the parts of a feather. Pacific silverweed was known to several coastal Indian tribes who used the root for food after it was steamed and dipped in whale oil.

BEACH PEA   *Lathyrus japonicus*   Pea Family

Found tangled amid the grasses of the foredune and along sandy beaches from Alaska to northern California, beach pea has inch-long purple or rose colored flowers and dark green pinnately compound leaves. The trailing stems grow up to 3 feet long. Beach pea spreads by rhizomes—creeping underground stems. These hold the plant securely in the loose sand. New shoots sprout from this underground stem, forming a new plant.

This group of the pea family is distinguished by their one-sided racemes of flowers (resembling those of the garden sweet pea) and pinnately compound leaves which usually have tendrils (a slender piece of stem or leaf that coils around other plants or objects for support).

GRAY BEACH PEA   *Lathyrus littoralis*   Pea Family

Gray beach pea may be found on foredunes and partially stabilized dunes where its prostrate, sprawling stems are partially hidden by the more upright stems of the beach grass. The leaves have a silky appearance due to their covering of soft hairs. The flowers grade in color from white to pink or purple. Although the *Lathyrus* group normally has tendrils at the tips of their pinnately-compound leaves, in this species the tendrils have been replaced by green appendages. Another name for this plant is Chinook licorice, referring to the use of this plant by coastal Indians who ate the roasted root.

TREE LUPINE   *Lupinus arboreus*   Pea Family

Tree lupine colors dunes and other sandy spots during the early summer with its golden yellow plumes of flowers. A woody shrub 3 to 5 feet tall, it lines coastal roadways and bays. Like other lupines, it has palmately compound leaves and clusters of pea-shaped flowers. *Arboreus* means tree-like; however, the branching main trunk makes it quite bushy. Growing readily from seed, it flowers after the second or third year and is a most attractive shrub. Native to the central California coast, it has been widely planted for dune stabilization and is now found along most of the Pacific Coast. It has also been introduced into other parts of the world for this purpose.

SEASHORE LUPINE   *Lupinus littoralis*   Pea Family

Lupines are showy members of the pea family. They have pea-shaped flowers that are borne in a raceme—a cluster of flowers, each with its own stalk, arranged along a central stem with the lower lateral flowers blooming before the ones at the tip. Lupines are usually identified by the palmately compound leaves—the leaflets spread from a common point, like the fingers of a hand. Although many individual lupines are difficult to distinguish from each other, the group as a whole is fairly easy to recognize.

A long, thick taproot holds seaside lupine in place so well that sand often blows out from around the plant, leaving it on a low mound or hummock. Some plants resemble a small, sprawling shrub 1 to 2 feet high, while other seaside lupine stems are prostrate, stretching over the sand. The flowers are pale blue. You'll find this lupine in a variety of places, from open dunes to sandy bluffs—but it is never far from the shore. It occurs from British Columbia to northern California.

26

GIANT VETCH   *Vicia gigantea*   Pea Family

You'll find giant vetch spreading and crawling over piles of driftwood debris at the edge of the beach. Look for it as you travel the Pacific Coast anywhere from Alaska to northern California. The stout, climbing stems are 3 to 6 feet long and have pinnately compound leaves of 16 to 30 leaflets. A fine, slender tendril aids giant vetch's spread by coiling around other plants or pieces of driftwood. The flowers are reddish-purple or bronze, about an inch long. They are borne in linear clusters.

The Pea Family is an extremely important economic group, including such food sources as the bean, soybean, pea, alfalfa, and peanut as well as many ornamentals such as the lupine, sweet pea, acacia, and redbud.

BEACH EVENING PRIMROSE   *Oenothera contorta*   Evening Primrose Family

This fleshy-leaved prostrate plant can be found on beaches and dunes from British Columbia south into California. Its stout stems stretch out across the surface of the sand, radiating from a leafy rosette. The thick leaves have a slightly gray color. The four-petaled flowers are about an inch across. They are bright yellow when they first open, but may turn pink or red with age. This evening primrose is barely a few inches tall, although the sprawling stems may be a foot or more long.

BEACH SILVERTOP   *Glehnia leiocarpa*   Parsley Family

Beach silvertop forms compact little clumps on beaches and dune areas, especially where sand has not yet become stabilized. A prostrate plant, it is characterized by compound, leathery leaves that are quite woolly on the lower surface; tight, round clusters of tiny white flowers; and balls of corky-winged fruit. Because it thrives in areas of drifting sand, beach silvertop quite often appears stemless, with even the sheathing leaf stems partially buried in the sand. In actuality, it is deeply rooted in the unstable sand by a stout taproot. The lower stem and leaves have adapted to the changing sand level and can withstand alternate burying and exposure by the sand and wind. The flowers begin to bloom during the early part of the summer and a given plant often bears flowers until the end of the season. Therefore, it is possible to find both flowers and fruit on the same plant in August. Look for beach silvertop along the coast from Alaska to northern California.

BEACH MORNING GLORY   *Convolvulus soldanella*   Morning Glory Family

Trailing its two-foot long stems across the sand of open beaches and dunes, beach morning glory is recognized by its fleshy, kidney-shaped leaves and trumpet-shaped pink or white flowers which are about 2 inches long. These bloom throughout the summer, but sometimes fail to open on a cloudy day. This morning glory helps bind the sand and seems to flourish where sand has not been stabilized. Many of the morning glories of the Northwest are actually native to other parts of the world and were introduced here. Beach morning glory is an exception and is native to the dunes of the Pacific Coast, from British Columbia to southern California.

SILVERY PHACELIA   *Phacelia argentea*   Waterleaf Family

Silvery phacelia is well-named. The stiff, white hairs covering the leaves produce a silvery effect in the sunlight. A stout perennial plant, this phacelia has round or oval leaves and dense clusters of white or pale yellow flowers. These are in round scorpioid heads, meaning the flowers are along a coiled or curved stem. Silvery phacelia grows 4 to 12 inches tall and blooms during the early summer, although a few blossoms may be found through August. Growing in sandy waysides, this phacelia occurs along the southern Oregon and northern California coasts.

BEACH SILVERWEED   *Ambrosia chamissonis*   Composite Family

Also called silver bursage or beach-bur. Beach silverweed might escape notice because its flowers are not particularly conspicuous or colorful. The large mats of silvery-green leaves, however, catch one's eye. They form little hummocks on open beaches and dunes. The prostrate stems grow from a large taproot and are between 2 and 4 feet long. Short white hairs cover the thick, spatulate leaves, giving them a silvery appearance. The tassel of flowers at the tips of the branches produce the pollen, while the seed-producing flowers are usually found in the leaf axils along the length of the stem or are clustered at the base of the pollen-bearing cluster of flowers. The plant blooms in July and the fruits appear in August and September. These are prickle-covered burrs. Beach silverweed is strictly a coastal plant and is found from Vancouver Island to central California.

BEACH GUMWEED   *Grindelia integrifolia*   Composite Family

Gumweed is best recognized by the cup-shaped base of the flower head, the outward-curving bracts that appear to have been coated with varnish, and the gummy substance associated with the flower head. In fact, when a new flower head opens, it is almost completely covered by this sticky, white material. The large yellow floral head (2 inches across is not uncommon) consists of both ray and disk flowers. Gumweed grows 2 to 3 feet tall and each plant contains many showy flower heads, so a cluster of these leafy plants is quite striking. Look for it along open beaches and salt marshes from southern Alaska to northern California. Gumweed blooms in August and September, although in some northern locations it may still be seen blooming in early October.

33

CAT'S EAR   *Hypochaeris radicata*   Composite Family

Easily mistaken for the common dandelion (*Taraxacum officinale*), cat's ear dots deflation plains and disturbed sandy places with its abundance of yellow flowers. All the leaves, which are irregularly toothed along the edges, are basal and covered with stiff, short hairs. The flowering stems are 6 to 24 inches tall and usually branch to bear more than one flowering head.

Cat's ear could be confused with hawkbit (*Leontodon nudicaulis*). It, too, has basal leaves and dandelion-like flower heads. The leaves form a dense rosette that is flattened against the sand. The flowering stems, however, are unbranched, each bearing a single flower head. It is a much smaller plant, the flowering stems rarely exceeding 6 inches.

All three of these plants are native to Europe and are generally considered weeds. Indeed, they invade lawns, pastures, and gardens where they can be serious pests. Amid the dune grasses, however, they have become naturalized and add a bit of color.

SEASIDE TANSY   *Tanacetum douglasii*   Composite Family

Also called western tansy. This stout-stemmed plant grows in open dunes and sandy flats, sometimes forming hummocks. The leaves are finely divided, almost fern-like, and have fine white hairs. The half-inch wide flower heads lack ray flowers and resemble pale yellow buttons. These are quite numerous and are located at the end of the stems. Where tansy has formed hummocks on the sand, it looks like a yellow-flowered bush. It grows along the coast from British Columbia to northern California.

Wetlands

WAX MYRTLE   *Myrica californica*   Sweet Gale Family

A shrub or small tree between 3 to 30 feet tall, wax myrtle is recognized by its shiny green, leathery, evergreen leaves and its clusters of nut-like, wax-covered fruits. The flowers are quite inconspicuous—tiny, green catkins. It is the waxy fruit that is noticeable. The four inch elliptic leaves have finely serrated margins. Common along the coast from central Washington to California, wax myrtle landscapes many campgrounds and picnic areas.

The family is recognized by the aromatic fragrance exuded from its leaves when they are crushed or bruised. These coastal shrubs are related to several well-known spices, including cloves and allspice.

YELLOW POND LILY   *Nuphar polysepalum*   Water-lily Family

These yellow bowl-shaped flowers adorn many of the sloughs and inter-tidal and inter-dunal ponds and lakes of the Pacific Coast. A thick rootstock anchors the yellow pond lily to the mud below and large leaves float alongside. These leaves themselves are conspicuous. They are rounded, heart-shaped at their base and often 12 inches or more across. Yellow pond lily is widespread in western North America.

This plant was known by the inland Klamath Indians as wokas and was harvested from dugouts. The ripened pods were pulled from their stems, stored, dried and roasted. The gathering of the wokas seed involved much celebrating among the Klamaths. Coastal Indians, however, also used this plant medicinally. The Quinault gathered the roots along the river, heated them, and applied them for pain relief, especially rheumatism. This aquatic plant is valuable today to a vast number of aquatic insects and other small creatures that seek shelter under the protective leaves. You will also find insect eggs attached to the underside. Here the eggs are kept moist while incubating and the newly hatched insects have a ready food supply. In turn, many birds frequent the pond lily while feeding on these insects.

SMALL CREEPING BUTTERCUP   *Ranunculus flammula*   Buttercup Family

Many of our native buttercups attract our attention because of their large yellow blossoms, which adorn roadsides and fields. Small creeping buttercup, however, maintains a low profile, growing only a few inches high. Its stems sprawl over sandy swales and send out roots at the leafy joints. The five-petaled flowers are quite small, barely a half inch wide. It grows in much of North America. Along the Pacific Coast, you'll find it occupying wet deflation plains between coastal dunes and the mudflats bordering estuaries.

The deflation plain is an area unique to coastal dunes. It is formed when wind blows sand away, removing it until the water table is reached. Often, they are completely covered with water during the winter months and are important stopping places for migrating waterfowl. Many birds that spend the summer breeding season in Alaska and northern Canada winter in these wet, coastal areas. By early summer much of the water is gone and the area merely damp. Then it is covered with a wide variety of small wildflowers and flowering shrubs. Small creeping buttercup shares deflation plains with Labrador tea, sundew, marsh clover, golden-eyed grass, gentian, and many other wildflowers. By late August, however, the water table has usually dropped so far that only dry sand, rushes, sedges, and leafy shrubs are easily seen.

CREEPING BUTTERCUP   *Ranunculus repens*   Buttercup Family

A native of Europe, creeping buttercup is now widely established throughout North America, and is fairly common along the Pacific Coast where it occurs in seeps and along roadside ditches. Its bright, golden-yellow saucer-shaped flowers, for instance, are common along U.S. 101 through Olympic National Park. Creeping buttercup grows about 12 inches high. Although the stems are prostrate near the base, their ability to root at the nodes often creates a tufted appearance. Its basal leaves are usually divided into three lobed leaflets. Additional linear leaves grow on the flowering stems. Sometimes, the leaves are dotted with white.

COBRA PLANT   *Darlingtonia californica*   Pitcher Plant Family

Scattered along the northern coast are small bogs, underlain with deposits of moisture-holding sphagnum. Here may be found some very interesting and unique plants. Some bogs are open and sunny, looking at first like wet meadows. Others are partially shaded. Some may be merely soggy or spongey and dry out by the end of the summer.

One of the most interesting plants growing in these bogs is the cobra plant. It has tubular, pitcher-like leaves which are enlarged above into a hood. These leaves are partially filled with enzymatic fluid which aids in the digestion or disintegration of insects and other small creatures that become trapped within. These leaves are 1 to 2 feet tall. In the early summer a flowering stalk appears, extending about 6 inches higher than the leaves and bearing a single nodding flower with 5 purple petals and 5 yellow sepals. The cobra plant gets its name because of the appearance of the upper portion of the pitcher-like leaves. Another common name for it is pitcher plant.

SUNDEW   *Drosera rotundifolia*   Sundew Family

Sundews are lowly plants, barely a few inches across. Their small size makes them easily overlooked. Once seen, however, they can be mistaken for no other native plant. Their round leaves form a rosette that hugs the damp ground. Indeed, to get a good look at them you must not only get your feet but also your knees wet. These little leaves are covered with sticky gland-tipped hairs in which small insects such as gnats and mosquitoes become entrapped. The moist appearance given the leaves by these secreting glands undoubtedly resulted in the common name since the leaf seems perpetually laden with dew. Once an insect has landed on the leaf, the small hairs tip inward and the insect is digested by enzymes secreted by the leaf. Even less frequently seen than the plant itself are the tiny white flowers which are borne on slender 5 or 6 inch tall stems. Sundews may grow in the soggy edge of a marsh or lake, in a coastal bog, or in a perpetually moist deflation plain.

Both the sundew and cobra plant are sometimes called insectivorous or carnivorous plants because they absorb nutrients from small insects or other animal material. These plants grow in sites such as bogs where the normal soil nutrients are either deficient or simply difficult to absorb from the soil. The extra nutrients derived this way help these plants to survive.

BURNET   *Sanguisorba officinalis*   Rose Family

Burnet grows in bogs and marshes along the coast, often in the company of tofieldia, camas, and bog laurel. Burnet is not conspicuous because of its individual flowers. Rather, it is the effect of their rose or purple colored blossoms grouped together at the end of the stems in oblong clusters, somewhat resembling a head of grain, that catches your eye. These flower clusters are 1 to 2 inches long and are on stems 4 to 24 inches tall. The pinnately compound leaves have toothed leaflets and are hidden amid the other marsh vegetation. While burnet may not be very common, it is plentiful in local areas where it does occur. Thus, the overall effect can be very striking: the burnt red clusters of flowers waving above the marsh grasses and sedges. It occurs from Alaska south along the coast and in the mountains to northwestern California and is also found in northern Eurasia.

DOUGLAS SPIREA   *Spiraea douglasii*   Rose Family

Also called western spirea, hardhack, steeple-bush. A conspicuous, pink-flowered shrub commonly found along roadside ditches and lake margins, Douglas spirea is a beautiful little shrub. It occurs from southern Alaska south along the coast to northern California and inland to British Columbia and Idaho. Growing 3 to 6 feet tall, it has oblong, toothed leaves. The flowers bloom in mid-summer and are in pyramid-shaped clusters that appear fuzzy because the numerous stamens in each flower are longer than the other floral parts. The flowers are pleasantly scented and their fragrance further enhances the beauty of the plant.

BIRD'S FOOT TREFOIL   *Lotus corniculatus*   Pea Family

Bird's foot trefoil is a brightly colored plant that may be found in moist waste areas such as roadsides, ditches, pastures, and fields. Originally a European plant, it is now widely found in the Pacific Northwest and colors many coastal swales. Compact clusters of yellow flowers top the ten to twenty inch tall stems, which are as apt to lie along the ground as to be upright. The leaves appear to be sessile and have five hairy leaflets. The bright yellow flowers make a colorful display in mid-summer, giving way to slender pods later in the season.

45

MARSH CLOVER   *Trifolium wormskjoldii*   Pea Family

Also called spring-bank clover. Spreading by creeping rootstocks, marsh clover may grow erect, though more often it sprawls across the sand in sunny openings. It is noticeable mainly because of its round, showy clusters of flowers. These are purple or red, sometimes tipped in white. Marsh clover may be found along fresh or salt marshes or in sandy depressions and dunes, from British Columbia south to Mexico. It also occurs east to Idaho and Colorado.

Another clover that will be encountered along the southern Oregon coast and the California coast is sour clover (*Trifolium fucatum*). It is a yellow-flowered annual which turns red with age.

The clovers are distinctive herbs characterized by compound leaves of three leaflets and flowers that are clustered into tight heads or clusters. Many clovers are extremely important economically. They are grown for pasture and hay. Like the commercial varieties, native clovers are extremely rich in nutrients. Many small rodents, especially chipmunks and ground squirrels, feast on both the leaves and the blossoms. In addition, the nectar-rich flowers are utilized by many bees who pollinate the blossoms in return for the nectar. Hummingbirds are also frequent visitors to the clover, especially those with red flowers.

TINKER'S PENNY *Hypericum anagalloides* St. John's Wort Family

If you trek into boggy spots or wet sandy areas, you may find yourself walking on tiny yellow flowers and glistening, dark green leaves. This is tinker's penny. Its slender stems either creep along the ground or stand erect. Even when erect, they are not very tall—usually only 6 inches or less. Half-inch, ovate leaves straddle the stems in pairs. The bright golden flowers are about one-half inch in diameter, and have 5 petals.

Because of the creeping nature of the stems, tinker's penny, also known as bog St. John's wort, may form a mat of brightly colored blossoms and shiny leaves, which always appear wet. This is mostly due to the small glistening glands on the leaves, not morning dew. However, if you plan to look for this dainty flower yourself, you should plan on getting your feet wet. It grows best where the ground is saturated. It occurs along the coast from British Columbia to Baja California and east to Montana.

The St. John's Wort Family is an interesting one, consisting of some brightly flowered ornamentals as well as some pesty weeds. According to superstition, the flowers of some species bloom on the day of the festival of St. John the Baptist, hence the name.

Tinker's penny adapts well to cool, moist garden nooks and makes a pleasant addition to a native garden.

WATER PARSLEY   *Oenanthe sarmentosa*   Parsley Family

Water parsley's prolific growth produces a pale white halo over many coastal marshes and roadside ditches. The stems grow up to 4 feet long and branch into a tangled mass. The compound leaves have coarsely-toothed leaflets. The tiny white flowers are borne in a tight, round-topped cluster called an umbel, characteristic of the parsley family.

As might be expected of a water plant, water parsley has thick, juicy stems. Because of its similarity to the poisonous water hemlock (*Cicuta douglasii*) no attempt should be made to eat or taste any part of this plant.

SWAMP LAUREL   *Kalmia polifolia*   Heath Family

This delicate-appearing and very beautiful shrub adorns boggy meadows. A low-growing shrub between 2 and 3 feet tall, it has oblong, evergreen leaves with inward rolled edges. The pale pink blossoms bloom during the early summer. The saucer-shaped flowers have five lobes and ten arched stamens radiating out from the center. Swamp laurel thrives in coastal bogs, usually in the company of Labrador tea, from Alaska to California. It also occurs in boggy mountain meadows throughout the western states. However, at these higher elevations it is a much smaller plant and grows only about 6 inches high.

49

LABRADOR TEA *Ledum glandulosum* Heath Family

Labrador tea graces coastal bogs and wet swales, sometimes forming a dense thicket. A beautiful shrub growing up to 4 feet tall, it has round-topped clusters of white flowers at the ends of the branches. The leathery, evergreen leaves have edges that are slightly rolled under. Their undersides are dotted with small glands, hence the specific name *glandulosum*. The leaves have a fragrant odor of their own, especially when bruised or crushed.

Closely related but more restricted to bogs is *Ledum groenlandicum*. Its leaf margins are strongly inrolled and you can tell the two species apart because the leaves of *Ledum groenlandicum* are densely covered with hairs on the underside.

SEA MILKWORT   *Glaux maritima*   Primrose Family

To find the delicate pink flowers of the sea milkwort, you must venture into salt water sloughs and tidewater flats. There it grows amid the reeds and sedges so common along coastal waterways. A fleshy plant, sea milkwort grows 10 to 12 inches tall and has pale pink, bell-shaped flowers tucked in the axils of the small, oblong leaves. A cosmopolitan plant, it is not only found in the coastal marshes of northern North America, but also those of Europe and Asia.

CENTAURY   *Centaurium umbellatum*   Gentian Family

Centaury dots deflation plains and other moist areas along the Pacific Coast. It grows 8 to 16 inches tall and has both tufted basal leaves and clasping elliptic stem leaves which are opposite each other. The deep pink or nearly purple flowers are in candelabra-like clusters. Each individual flower is tubular, with 5 widely-spreading lobes. Centaury's stem is square so that it does not roll easily in your fingers. Blooming throughout July and August, centaury grows in the company of sundew, labrador tea, gentian, willow, and other plants that require moist ground. Introduced from Europe, it is now widely established in the Pacific Northwest where it is found in moist wastelands, meadows, and swales.

COMMON GENTIAN   *Gentiana sceptrum*   Gentian Family

Also called staff gentian, king's gentian. Growing in wet deflation plains that stay moist through most of the summer and in coastal bogs, this gentian does not unfold its glorious blue flowers until late August. Funnel-shaped, the flower lobes scarcely appear to open even then. One to two inches long, the flowers top plants that grow 8 to 28 inches tall and have opposite leaves along the entire length of the stem.

A wet meadow or bog that is covered with blooming gentian is a beautiful sight. By this time the rushes and sedges have begun to turn brown or gold; the camas has replaced its blue flowers with pods of seeds, and the willow leaves have been gnawed by insects. The deep blue of the gentian lends a splash of color to the more subtle gold hues at the end of the growing season. Look for it along the Pacific Coast from British Columbia to northern California.

WILD MINT   *Mentha arvensis*   Mint Family

A fragrant herb, wild mint can be found in the deflation plains of the Clatsop Spit and in other marshes and damp spots along the coast. The leafy stems are 10 to 20 inches tall and the round clusters of pale purple flowers are tucked in the axils of the leaves along the upper portion of the plant. Often suckers emerge from the base of the plant, resulting in a bushy appearance. This mint occurs across most of North America.

You can smell the minty fragrance of this plant as you approach it. An even stronger scent is obtained if you crush a leaf. Take the stem in your fingers. It is not round, but square, and therefore does not roll very easily. Square stems are characteristic of the entire mint family.

COMMON MONKEYFLOWER   *Mimulus guttatus*   Figwort Family

These bright yellow flowers are found in moist swales and along stream banks. Resembling the garden snapdragon, each flower is a two-lipped basket. The lower lip is the larger and is generally divided into three shallow lobes. Often there are spots of brown, red, purple, or maroon in the throat of the flower. Growing 2 to 24 inches tall, monkeyflower has round, irregularly lobed leaves. This monkeyflower is capable of reproducing with runners or small shoots that sprout from the base. This trait makes it especially conspicuous when it grows in moist sandy places. The runners often sprout along the waterline of a wet swale, resulting in a line of monkeyflowers that resembles a planted row.

Common monkeyflower could be confused with coast monkeyflower (*Mimulus dentatus*) which is found in deflation plains and swales. It, too, has yellow flowers with purple-dotted throats. In both species the leaves are opposite but in coast monkeyflower, the leaves are distinctly pinnately veined, while those of common monkeyflower are usually palmately veined.

55

FIGWORT   *Scrophularia californica*   Figwort Family

Many travelers fail to recognize the figwort as a wildflower. Its maroon or brown flowers
are only about one-half inch long and easily escape notice. The plant, itself, however, is
quite tall, growing up to two to five feet. It is a rather coarse-appearing plant, and is found
amid the rank growth in brushy and damp places along the coast, from Vancouver Island
to southern California. The flowers, each a small, two-lipped basket, are in loose panicles
(a flower cluster with branched stems) at the top of the plant. The leaves are opposite
each other on the stem and toothed along their margins. Figwort blooms from March
through July.

BEARBERRY HONEYSUCKLE   *Lonicera involucrata*   Honeysuckle Family

Also called twinberry, bush honeysuckle, ink-berry. A shrubby bush with simple, opposite leaves, this honeysuckle has tubular yellow flowers that are sometimes tinged with pink or red. These occur in pairs, cupped in a leaf-like dark red bract and attached to the leaf axil by a long stem. The bracts become even more conspicuous when the flowers fade and are replaced by blue-black berries. It is the dark color of the berries that account for the common name ink-berry. In fact, the ink colored juice from these berries was used as a dye by some of the coastal Indians. Found in moist spots along streams or in marshy areas throughout most of North America, bearberry honeysuckle blooms from March to May.

BRASS BUTTONS   *Cotula coronopifolia*   Composite Family

These yellow flower heads deserve their common name; indeed they do resemble buttons. The low-growing plant has stems that are barely 12 inches long and may be almost prostrate. The oblong leaves clasp the stem and the lower ones may be deeply cleft. The flower heads, about one-half inch wide, are flattened but slightly raised in the center. There are no ray flowers, the compact disk being formed by tubular flowers. Brass buttons may be found blooming in tidal marshes, wet beaches, deflation plains, and bogs. The flowers appear during the early part of the summer.

A native of South Africa, brass buttons now grows along most of the Pacific Coast from British Columbia through California, as well as along the Atlantic Coast of North America and in the southern hemisphere.

58

JAUMEA   *Jaumea carnosa*   Composite Family

Jaumea's succulent leaves and stems spread horizontally across the ground, forming a loose mat. The narrow leaves are opposite each other, clasping the stem at the base. A single yellow flower head is on its own somewhat erect stem, which is 3 to 4 inches tall. Jaumea blooms from June through October. Look for it in tidal areas, usually sprawled across the inlets and peninsulas carved by the ebb and flow of the ocean from Vancouver Island to southern California.

Coastal shores near estuaries and bays often have flat areas where silt has been deposited over time. These may form extensive mudflats that are alternately flooded and exposed by the changing tides. The flush of sea water brings with it the tiny plant and animal life that makes these areas so rich. Plants that live on these shores must adapt to the alternating tides. For part of each day they are bathed in salt water and must have strong root systems to hold them in place against the surging stream of the ocean. They must also have a tough surface on their stems and leaves to withstand the penetrating salt of sea water.

A small genus of only about 9 species, Jaumea has only this representative on our Pacific Coast. Other members of this genus occur in Mexico, South America, and Africa.

CAT-TAIL   *Typha latifolia*   Cat-Tail Family

The cat-tail is familiar to most of us. It grows from Alaska to Mexico, occurs in most of southern Canada and extends into Eastern United States. It can also be found in northern Africa and most of Eurasia. Cat-tails grow in shallow water, often to the exclusion of most other plants. You'll find it bordering shallow coastal lakes and marshes. The long, narrow leaves grow in a sheath around the flowering stems, which are between 4 and 10 feet tall. The pollen-bearing (or male) flowers and seed-producing (or female) flowers are separated on the flowering stalk. The smaller brown flowers at the top of each stalk are the pollen-bearers; the large, thickened flowers are the seed-producers which, by the end of the summer, begin to break apart from the stalk, exuding their puffy plumes of seeds.

The pollen can be used as flour, the upper spike can be eaten in its bud stage as a vegetable, young shoots can be used as salad greens, and the root substitutes as a potato-like food. In light of these facts, it is interesting to note that Northwest coastal Indians did not consider the cat-tail a primary food item. It was most often gathered as weaving material. Cat-tail leaves provided kneeling mats for canoes, screens for winter homes, and roof material for temporary or summer dwellings. Pack sacks and baskets were also made of this material. Perhaps the prime value of cat-tails today is as shelter and nesting sites for a large number of birds and other marsh wildlife.

SKUNK CABBAGE *Lysichitum americanum* Arum Family

One of the first signs of spring along the coast is the appearance of the yellow hoods of skunk cabbage. They fill swales and waterways and even occur in otherwise well-groomed pastures. Although skunk cabbage also occurs inland, it is most conspicuous along the Pacific coastal strip. The brightly-colored hood (botanically known as a spathe) encloses the skunk cabbage flowers, which are clustered at the upper end of a foot-tall stalk. The floral stalk eventually outgrows the protective yellow hood and by mid or late summer, large green cabbage-like leaves are all that remain. These are a dark green and grow up to 3 feet tall and 1 foot wide. The common name comes from the odor released by the leaves when they are bruised or crushed.

Coastal Indians used the skunk cabbage for a variety of purposes. The Quileute and Quinault were known to cook and eat the roots. In the spring when other food was scarce, skunk cabbage roots were probably easy to gather because the soil was soft. It was evidently not a favorite food because of its strong scent. The large leaves were used as baskets for gathering and drying salal and elderberries. Bear are also fond of skunk cabbage, eating leaves, roots, and fruits. It is the root, however, that is most eagerly sought, especially in early spring.

61

COMMON CAMAS   *Camassia quamash*   Lily Family

The blue flowers of common camas dance above wet swales and bogs with the slightest coastal breeze. Camas has three sepals and three petals which all appear similar, making the flower appear to have six petals. Five of these are erect or horizontal while the sixth turns downward. (This distinguishes it from the other camas commonly found in the Northwest, Leichtlin's camas, *Camassia leichtlinii*, which has these six floral parts arranged symmetrically.) Common camas grows 12 to 24 inches tall and has grasslike leaves, making it blend well with the sedges and grasses of the areas where it grows.

Camas bulbs were important articles in the diet of Northwestern Indians. The bulbs were usually dug in late summer after the plant had gone to seed.

GOLDEN-EYED GRASS   *Sisyrinchium californicum*   Iris Family

The buttery-yellow flowers of this petite little plant dot wet, sandy places in dunes, coastal swales, bog borders, and lake margins, from Vancouver Island to southern California. The stout, flattened stems grow about 12 inches tall and have somewhat shorter, iris-like basal leaves. The flowers of this genus have three sepals and three petals that are very similar and look alike. They are often mistaken for lilies. The dainty flowers are about one-half inch across.

While golden-eyed grass is restricted to areas west of the Cascades, blue-eyed grass (*Sisyrinchium angustifolium*) is quite widespread in the western United States. With similar leaves and stature, its flowers, however, are purple with yellow centers. Along the coast these two plants often grow side by side in wet spots. Blue-eyed grass is also found on grassy slopes which are still damp in early springtime.

The Iris Family is well-known and loved, largely because of the large-flowered cultivated members of the group. The smaller members of the family contained in the Sisyrinchium genus display the basic features of Iris even though their flowers may superficially resemble those of the lily. Look for the smooth stems. Because of the arrangement of the ensheathing leaves at the base, they will appear to be flattened.

63

STREAM ORCHIS   *Epipactus gigantea*   Orchid Family

Occurring along stream banks and in moist swales, this wildflower eludes many hikers, even though it is widespread in the Pacific Northwest. Ornately designed, the green and purple flowers nonetheless blend into the surrounding vegetation. Growing from 1 to 3 feet tall, stream orchis has large (2 to 6 inches long), ovate leaves. Its flowers are arranged loosely along the upper portion of the stem. These flowers are typical of the orchid group: each is irregularly-shaped, with three sepals and three petals. Two of these petals are alike; the third is called the lip and may be slipper-shaped, bulbous, strap-shaped, tubular, or otherwise variously shaped. It is this third petal that gives the orchid flower its unique shape. The lip of the stream orchid is concave at the base and spreads out at the tip.

The tropical climates of the world are known for their large and beautiful orchids. Many are surprised to find that a wide variety of orchids also grow in the temperate portions of North America. Although the flowers of our native orchids are usually small and inconspicuous, close examination reveals the delicate structures and beautiful patterns and colors of the most lavish tropical varieties.

64

SLENDER BOG ORCHID *Habenaria saccata* Orchid Family

A spike of small green flowers helps identify this native orchid. Bog orchid has leafy stems 12 to 36 inches tall. The linear leaves occur along the entire length of the stem, but are much reduced toward the upper portion. It can be found in swampy and boggy places along the Pacific Coast from Alaska to southern Oregon. It also occurs inland across western North America. The bog orchid has the characteristic design of orchid flowers. Each flower consists of 3 petals and 3 sepals. The third petal causes the irregular shape of the flower and is called the lip. The lip in slender bog orchid is flat and fashioned into a swollen, sack-shaped spur.

LADIES' TRESSES   *Spiranthes romanzoffiana*   Orchid Family

Resembling the finely braided hair of a well-coiffeured lady, the greenish-white flowers of this little orchid form a spiral twist atop a 6 to 24 inch tall stem. The genus name *Spiranthes* refers to this trait, being derived from the Greek words meaning coil and flower. You'll find ladies' tresses in wet deflation plains and swales behind the beach from Alaska to southern California. They also occur inland across northern North America. Along our Pacific Coast they bloom in late July and August. Since most specimens are only about 10 to 12 inches tall, you will have to get down on hands and knees to see one closely.

Cliffs / Grasslands

FIELD CHICKWEED *Cerastium arvense* Pink Family

These showy, white flowers, often with petals nearly an inch long, grow on bluffs and beaches along the coast. The deeply notched petals produce an ornate appearance. Several stems 3 to 20 inches tall emerge from the plant base, giving chickweed a tufted appearance. The lance-shaped leaves are glandular, making them slightly sticky. Chickweed blooms from May through August, so you are apt to find it no matter when you visit the coast. A good place to look for it is on the bluffs and sea stacks along the Olympic Peninsula. Field chickweed is an exotic and has become widespread in North America.

The field chickweed is a widely ranging species which can vary greatly from one area to another. Those found along the coast are usually densely hairy, especially along the upper portion of the plant. Those found at higher mountainous areas are less hairy and tend to have broader leaves than the coastal plants.

Chickweed belongs to the large and varied Pink Family, a group of herbs with opposite leaves and symmetrical, often showy flowers. It is a large group, with perhaps as many as 2,000 species. Most of these occur in the Northern Temperate Zone. The Pink Family includes many weedy species but also has many beautiful ornamentals that are common garden flowers—the sandworts, garden pink, campion, and catchfly are examples.

COLUMBINE   *Aquilegia formosa*   Buttercup Family

The columbine is one of the more common and beloved wildflowers in the Northwest. It is also one of our most beautiful. A 2 to 4 foot tall stem supports the showy, nodding flowers. These are formed from five prolonged petals that are turned backward and upward to form crimson spurs or sacs, while the forward portions form yellow blades. This columbine can be found from sea level nearly to timberline in the Pacific States and also in the Rocky Mountains. It grows in a variety of soil types but does best along stream banks and moist woodland borders. The colorful blossoms appear in April and May and a few can usually still be found toward the end of the summer.

This columbine provides a charming addition to flower gardens and is very easy to start from seed. You can collect the seeds in late summer and plant them in mid-winter. They will not bloom until the second summer, but then will provide color for your garden for many years to come.

FIELD LARKSPUR   *Delphinium menziesii*   Buttercup Family

Larkspurs range over much of North America. Many kinds are difficult to tell apart. However, the group as a whole is easy to identify. They are herbaceous plants with palmately lobed leaves and irregularly shaped purple flowers that are in clusters at the upper tip of the flowering stem. A long, backward-protruding spur is formed by one of the sepals. It is this distinctive flower shape that makes larkspurs easy to identify.

This species, which grows up to 24 inches tall, has leaves that are deeply cleft into 3 to 5 main parts and these are divided again. Even though the basal leaves are deeply cleft, they have a round outline. Only a few flowers are clustered at the tip of each stem. These are a dark purple, except for the upper petals which are usually white or lined with purple. Look for it on coastal bluffs, where it may be found in the company of the wallflower, cow parsnip, and tiger lily.

70

FIELD BUTTERCUP *Ranunculus occidentalis* Buttercup Family

Buttercups are among the most common and well-known wildflowers. They are recognized by their shiny or waxy yellow petals, which usually number five. Two species common in damp sites are referred to elsewhere in this book. Two species found among the grasses of coastal headlands, meadows, and fields and often encountered along the Pacific Coast are the western or field buttercup and California buttercup.

Field buttercup has several stems 4 to 20 inches tall. The lower leaves are usually three-lobed, each lobe again being shallowly lobed or toothed. The yellow flowers have five narrow petals and are about an inch in diameter. California buttercup (*Ranunculus californicus*) is easily recognized because it deviates from the normal pattern of five petals and, instead, has eight to sixteen petals on each flower.

A widespread and variable group of wildflowers, the buttercup family also boasts many ornamental garden plants such as the anemone, columbine, larkspur, and peony.

71

OREGON GRAPE   *Berberis nervosa*   Barberry Family

Also known as mahonia, barberry, holly grape, and long leaved Oregon grape. These bright golden flowers may be found in late April, May and June on open bluffs and forest borders from British Columbia to central California. You'll recognize the shiny leaves of 11 to 21 holly-shaped leaflets. Growing up to 3 feet tall, this species spreads readily from underground, horizontal stems. It is quite a bit smaller than the Oregon grape known as the state flower of Oregon (*Berberis aquifolium*). The latter species, common in inland foothills, grows up to 6 feet tall and has leaves with 5 to 9 leaflets. Both species have purple berries by the latter part of the summer.

Both Oregon grapes were widely used by coastal Indians. The yellowish inner bark was used extensively for dyeing various weaving materials for baskets, mats and even clothing. Later Indians used the dye for coloring rag rugs. The berries were also gathered by many Indians who ate them, both raw and cooked. However, there were exceptions. The Maka, who lived along the Straits of Juan deFuca, regarded the berries as mere raven food, not to be eaten by members of their tribe.

72

CALIFORNIA POPPY   *Eschscholtzia californica*   Poppy Family

California poppy is a common sight along roadside bluffs and coastal fields, especially in southern Oregon and northern California. Originally found from the Columbia River to southern California, it is becoming established along the Washington and British Columbia Coasts as well. It sprouts easily from seed and has been introduced into many places as a garden flower. It has been quick to sprout in dry fields and meadows.

Poppy plants grow about a foot tall and have finely dissected leaves that are an attractive blue-green color. The large showy flowers have four petals that may be a golden yellow or a crimson orange. When the buds first appear, the outer flower parts form a pointed cap which is pushed off as the petals unfold. The flowers appear with the warm weather of May and may persist through the summer, especially where the mild coastal climate allows a second crop of these colorful annuals from an early seed crop. A sun-loving plant, its flowers close at night. On cloudy days they may open only partially or not at all.

WALLFLOWER   *Erysimum asperum*   Mustard Family

The orange and yellow of wallflowers add bright color to rocky cliffs and grassy bluffs. This wallflower is a stout, coarse plant that may be found blooming on many of the basalt headlands along the central Pacific coast. The stems grow 1 to 3 feet tall and are somewhat hairy. Narrow, linear leaves extend along the stem and are 3 to 6 inches long. It is the cluster of flowers, however, that attract attention. It is round-topped, 3 to 4 inches in diameter, and consists of bright orange, burnt red, yellow or maroon flowers. It is widespread in western North America.

The mustard group is fairly large, containing a variable assortment of plants. Some, like the cabbage, turnip, and radish, are of economic value. Others are more often thought of as weeds, growing along roadsides and in abandoned fields. As a group they are identified by alternate leaves, and a characteristic flower. There are four sepals and four petals, which spread opposite each other to form a cross—the Latin name for the family is Cruciferae, referring to the cross formed by the opposite petals. There are six stamens, two of which are shorter than the other four. This floral pattern is typical of mustard flowers and helps you identify the group.

OREGON STONECROP   *Sedum oreganum*   Stonecrop Family

Rocky basalt cliffs along the coast are often splattered with yellow color in early summer. Close inspection reveals the small, star-shaped flowers and rounded, succulent leaves of Oregon stonecrop, sometimes called western stonecrop. Trailing across the rocky nooks and crannies with matted and branching rootstocks, this stonecrop has leafy shoots terminated by tight rosettes. The rounded leaves are often tinged with hues of bronze, especially toward the end of summer. The flowering stems are about four inches tall. They have bright yellow flowers, each with five petals that are fused at the base. Oregon stonecrop occurs from British Columbia to California.

Found on well-drained sites, stonecrop has leaves that absorb and store water when it is plentiful. Then, during times of drought, the plant can utilize this stored moisture. This feature is advantageous along the Pacific Coast where summers are often dry and the thin mantle of soil covering rocky headlands holds little moisture.

The Stonecrop Family contains about 1500 species of plants. It consists of herbs and small shrubs with succulent or fleshy leaves and regular (symmetrical) flowers. The family contains many plants that are used widely for garden borders and in rock gardens. Many are cultivated specifically for landscaping. The attractive foliage makes them excellent garden plants year around.

75

BROAD-LEAVED STONECROP   *Sedum spatulifolium*   Stonecrop Family

Broad-leaved stonecrop might easily be confused with Oregon stonecrop. It, too, has star-shaped flowers and succulent leaves. However, its flowers are a pale yellow or cream color and the individual flower petals are completely separate. The leaves are distinctly spatulate in shape and the basal leaves form conspicuous rosettes. It grows on well-drained cliffs and hillsides from British Columbia to California.

Spectacular headlands of volcanic basalt dot much of the coastline. Often, forest communities dominate the cooler northern side of these headlands. Open rock and grassy slopes are found on the southern exposures and support a wide variety of wildflowers. The stonecrop thrives here. These headlands are excellent places to search for wildflowers in the spring and early summer. The moist soil of the southern slopes supports many grassland wildflowers and the forested northern slope harbors many shade-loving plants.

The coastal vegetation gradually changes as one travels southward. Forested slopes dominate the shoreline along Vancouver Island and the Washington coast. Basalt headlands punctuate the Oregon coast and their southern slopes are increasingly covered with grassland rather than forest. The northern California coast is dominated by these grassy slopes, with only a rare sprinkling of forest along the ocean.

The warmer, drier climate in the southern portion certainly influences this change. The general topography is probably another factor. Steep mountain slopes and bluffs immediately adjacent to the ocean are more common along the southern Oregon and northern California coasts.

76

OCEAN SPRAY   *Holodiscus discolor*   Rose Family

Also called arrow-wood and creambush. Closely resembling the foam thrown on shore by the stiff winds of a coastal storm, ocean spray is well-known by its thick plume of tightly clustered white flowers. A shrub 3 to 20 feet tall, it has wedge-shaped, simple leaves. (It could possibly be confused with goat's beard; however, the leaves of goat's beard are compound, divided two or three times.) Ocean spray blooms from May through July and is abundant on coastal bluffs, along streams, and in open woods. You'll find it in many of the campgrounds dotting the coast. It grows from British Columbia south through California and east in the mountains to western Montana.

Ocean spray is used as an ornamental and graces many Northwestern gardens. Indians had far more important uses for it, however. Widely used as shafts for arrows, it was known as "ironwood" by many tribes. The hard wood was used for digging sticks, campfire prongs, canoe paddles, and many other wooden utensils.

77

BLUFF MALLOW   *Sidalcea hirtipes*   Mallow Family

Found on coastal bluffs and grasslands, this mallow blooms in late June and early July along the Washington and northern Oregon coasts. A stout plant with hairy, leafy stems, it grows about 3 feet tall. The five-petalled pink or lavender flowers are clustered near the tip of the stems and make a conspicuous dash of color amid the rank grasses that surround it.

A similar species found in southern Oregon and California, checkerbloom (*Sidalcea malvaeflora*) may be a sprawling or erect plant. It, too, has rose or pink flowers, and grows on exposed, ocean-facing slopes.

The Mallow Family is widespread and contains many plants of economic value, cotton being one of the more important. The large, showy flowers of many species have made them popular in the garden as well—the hibiscus and the common hollyhock are included in this catagory.

HENDERSON'S ANGELICA   *Angelica hendersonii*   Parsley Family

Similar in general appearance to cow parsnip, angelicas grow along the edge of coastal beaches. Both plants have large clusters of white flowers, stout stems, and large compound leaves. Their main differences are subtle. Angelica fruits have winged ribs and the marginal flowers in each cluster are not enlarged. In cow parsnip only the lateral fruit ribs are winged and the marginal flowers in each floral cluster are larger than the center flowers.

Two angelicas can be seen along the northern Pacific coast. Henderson's angelica grows three to six feet tall and has stout, hollow stems. The pinnately compound leaves have petioles (leaf stems) that closely sheath the main stem. These leaves are green above, but covered by a dense coat of woolly hairs beneath. You'll find it from southern Washington to central California.

Seacoast angelica (*Angelica lucida*) is quite similar. However, its leaves lack the woolly covering on their undersides. Seacoast angelica grows along the entire length of the Pacific Coast as well as on the Atlantic and Siberian coasts.

WILD CARROT *Daucus carota* Parsley Family

By the end of summer the grasses of coastal headlands and fields turn a golden brown. Few flowers remain. The wild carrot, however, is in its prime, waving parasols of tiny white flowers in the breeze. All the flowers are white, except the center one which is a deep rose. From above, the round flower clusters resemble a carefully embroidered doily of lace 2 to 3 inches across. This pattern gives rise to another common name, Queen Anne's lace.

A stout, hairy plant with finely divided carrot-like leaves, it grows up to 3 feet tall. Wild carrot rises from a fleshy taproot, which plainly has a carrot odor. In fact, it is from this plant that all domestic carrots have been derived. Wild carrot is generally a biennial, meaning that during the first year only a clump of leaves appears close to the ground. Not until the second year does the flower stalk grow.

Wild carrot is originally a native of Europe, but has become widely established over much of North America. The native plant, American carrot (*Daucus pusillus*) is much smaller, barely reaching 12 inches in height. Its flower clusters are only about an inch across. An annual plant, it, too, is common in dry open places along the coast.

80

COW PARSNIP   *Heracleum lanatum*   Parsley Family

Cow parsnip is one of the most conspicuous members of the parsley family. Its large size makes it impossible to overlook. The stout stems grow 4 or 5 feet tall, although they occasionally grow up to 8 or 9 feet high. The stems are not the only large parts of this plant. The leaves, divided into 3 deeply toothed leaflets, are also large. They grow 3 to 10 inches across and their general shape resembles rhubarb. The white flowers are clustered into flat-topped heads 5 to 12 inches across. You'll find cow parsnip blooming in moist spots and grassy coastal slopes during the early part of the summer. It is not only common on the Pacific Coast but is widespread in North America and is also found in Siberia.

Coastal Indians sought out cow parsnip in the spring. The young tops were eaten raw. Also the stems were eaten later in the summer. Other variations included eating the young stems with seal oil. The ribs of the large flower clusters were used for making small baskets for the youngsters to play with.

The parsley family is well-represented in the coastal flora. The family is fairly distinctive. The flowers are in groupings called umbels, meaning the individual flower stems originate from a common point, much like the ribs of an umbrella. The relative length of these stems determines whether the flower cluster is flat-topped or rounded.

SPRING GOLD   *Lomatium utriculatum*   Parsley Family

One of the earliest plants to bloom in the spring, you can find the clusters of golden yellow flowers dotting well-drained slopes and bluffs in March, from British Columbia south to California. The leaves are dissected into many small lacy segments. The umbels of yellow flowers are tucked close to the ground. Spring gold continues to bloom through the spring months; however, the flowers are on taller stems (up to 12 inches tall) and tend to become lost amid the faster growing surrounding grasses. Since spring gold grows best on rocky bluffs, it usually commands scenic, windswept vistas. Whenever you find it, you will also be treated to an ocean view.

The Lomatium genus is known for its long taproot. Other members of this group are scattered across the northern Great Plains and in the Rocky, Cascade, and Sierra Nevada mountains. The Indians used the roots extensively for food and taught this use to early explorers and settlers. The journals of Lewis and Clark record buying Lomatium roots from local Indians as they traveled across America to the Pacific.

82

FOOTSTEPS-OF-SPRING   *Sanicula arctopoides*   Parsley Family

Also called beach snake-root and yellow-mats. Growing on exposed bluffs and beaches, from Vancouver Island south along the coast to southern California, footsteps-of-spring is well named. It blooms in March and April. Remaining low to the ground, its leaves and stems form a rosette-type arrangement about a foot across. The leaves are divided into three, deeply lobed segments. The rather inconspicuous yellow flowers are grouped in compact umbels, a flower arrangement that is typical of the parsley family. The foliage of footsteps-of-spring has a yellow-green tinge, allowing it to stand out a bit amid the fresh green foliage of most early spring plants.

The Parsley Family is a large and varied group, containing perhaps as many as 3,000 species of plants. Most of these are found in the drier and temperate climates of the world. Included are many plants with edible roots, seeds, and foliage. The carrot, parsley, parsnip, celery, caroway, and dill are good examples. However, the group also contains some weedy species and some very highly poisonous plants (such as poison hemlock). No wild plant should ever be eaten before it has been positively identified.

THRIFT   *Armeria maritima*   Leadwort Family

Also called sea-pink. Found on bluffs and sea terraces along the ocean, these compact, round clusters of pink flowers dance wildly in the sea breeze. The narrow leaves are tufted at the base of the flowering stem, which grows 4 to 20 inches tall. Sea pink blooms from April through August, so is seen by many coastal visitors; however, it is often overlooked because of its small size.

Thrift is not only found along the Pacific and Atlantic Coasts of North America, but also grows in northern Europe. In addition, it has found its way into many domestic yards as a charming addition to a rock garden.

84

BLUE GILIA   *Gilia capitata*   Phlox Family

Also called globe gilia because of the round floral clusters. An erect, annual plant, this gilia grows on open slopes and meadows along the coast from British Columbia to central California, as well as inland at lower elevations. The deep blue or lavender blossoms are in dense, round clusters (containing as many as 100 or more individual flowers) that are about an inch across. Blue gilia grows from 10 to 24 inches tall and has 1 to 4 inch long leaves, divided into deeply notched, narrow lobes.

The Gilia genus contains from 40 to 50 species of plants, over half of which occur in California. This gilia was first collected by the early botanical explorer, David Douglas, during his stay at Fort Vancouver. Douglas was one of the first botanists to travel and collect specimens in the Pacific states. Sent by the Horticultural Society of London, Douglas was stationed at the Hudson Bay Company's Ft. Vancouver from 1825 to 1827 and again in 1830. From there he traveled to Monterey, California, where he worked until 1832. During this time he sent a great number of seeds back to England. Native North American plants soon graced many English gardens.

SELF-HEAL   *Prunella vulgaris*   Mint Family

Self-heal is found in moist shaded areas or meadows and is widespread in North America. It grows 4 to 12 inches tall and has opposite oblong or ovate leaves that are 1 to 3 inches long. Small pink or purple flowers grow in dense terminal spikes that are an inch or more tall.

The name self-heal comes from its supposed value as a remedy for a variety of ailments, especially the common sore throat. Its ability to adapt to new conditions is reflected in the specific name vulgaris, meaning common. There are several sub-species. The native variety is an erect plant while the European variety that also occurs along the coast is dwarf or prostrate. It forms a blue carpet in the otherwise manicured lawns of several of our coastal state parks.

COAST PAINTBRUSH　　　　　*Castilleja litoralis*　　　　　Figwort Family

To see the flowers of paintbrush, one has to get down on hands and knees and look carefully. What appear to be the "flowers" are actually bracts, like the conspicuous part of the poinsetta and the dogwood. These bracts shelter the true blossoms. If you fold them back, you'll find small, tubular flowers that are two-lipped. They usually have subdued colors of green, orange, yellow, or red. It is the larger bract with its bright colors, that attracts attention and makes the paintbrush group so colorful.

Overlooking the ocean from basalt headlands, bluffs, and old dunes, coast paintbrush lends its beauty to rugged sections of the Pacific coastline from Washington to northern California. Blooming through most of the summer months, this is the most common paintbrush found along our coast. Its loosely clustered stems are woody at the base and grow 5 to 25 inches tall. The hairy bracts are tipped with scarlet, often with a band of yellow below. The flower itself, tucked within the bract, is pale green and red.

A yellow-bracted species found along the coast in the Puget Sound area and on Vancouver Island is golden Indian-paintbrush (*Castilleja levisecta*). It is generally found in swampy or moist places.

FOXGLOVE   *Digitalis purpurea*   Figwort Family

Foxglove is a beautiful, very conspicuous plant along roadsides and other recently disturbed areas. Growing 2 to 6 feet tall, its hairy leaves are toothed and oblong. Foxglove is a biennial, meaning that it requires two years to complete its life cycle. A rosette is formed during the first growing season; the flower-bearing stem appears the second year. It is the flowers that attract attention. They are basket-shaped from 1 to 2 inches long and are concentrated along the upper portion of the stem. Hanging downward, they are purple or sometimes white, with dark spots on the inner lining.

Foxglove is a native of Europe but was transported to North America by early settlers either as a garden plant or for its medicinal properties. An official drug plant, it was gathered extensively in Oregon and Washington during the first World War for treatment of heart ailments. Now, the drug is gathered from plants grown commercially. Foxglove readily covers logged-over areas and road banks with its purple color and also invades pastures, where it is considered a pest by farmers because it is toxic to livestock. It is common on the west side of the Cascade-Sierra Mountains from British Columbia to southern California.

WILD CUCUMBER   *Marah oreganus*   Gourd Family

Wild cucumber clamors over coastal vegetation, its thin tendrils (thin, coiling stems or modified leaves) attaching to other plants for support. The broad, rough-textured leaves are lobed and grow out from the long, vine-like stem. Wild cucumber blooms in April, May, and June. There are two types of flowers. The pollen-bearing flowers are in a long-stemmed cluster while the seed-bearing flower is solitary and is found in the leaf axil. The green fruit resembles a small round cucumber and is about three inches long. Its surface is covered with soft bristles.

Other common names for wild cucumber are bigroot and old-man-in-the-ground. These names refer to the large, woody root. Specimens weighing over twenty pounds have been found. It is the large size of this root that allows the rapid above-ground growth of wild cucumber in an area that has been recently cleared or otherwise disturbed. Look for it along the coast from southern British Columbia to California.

YARROW   *Achillea millefolium*   Composite Family

Yarrow grows in sandy openings and dunes; yarrow grows along roadsides and in other waste areas; yarrow grows at timberline in western mountains. Found throughout North America, yarrow is an extremely adaptable and widespread plant. It has erect stems 12 to 30 inches tall; however, where it is hit by constant salt spray and coastal winds, it may be much shorter and in small, tufted clumps. The strongly-scented leaves are divided into many small segments. The white or pale pink flowers are arranged in "heads" and consist of two basic types. The center of the head is composed of small tubular flowers; what appear to be individual petals are actually flowers, usually called ray or strap-shaped flowers. There are usually between four or five of these. The entire head looks like a single flower to the novice.

The Composite Family is entirely made up of flowers arranged in these or similar floral heads. Some types are made up entirely of strap or ray flowers—the common dandelion is one example, cat's ear is another. Others have only tubular flowers—chapparral broom and thistle are examples. Still others are like the yarrow and contain both types of flowers—aster, goldenrod, and daisy.

PEARLY EVERLASTING   *Anaphalis margaritacea*   Composite Family

Pearly everlasting is a bunched or loosely tufted plant of sand dunes and dry openings occurring in both North America and Eurasia. It grows 1 to 2 feet tall and has woolly white leaves. The flower heads are in tight, round-topped clusters that expand up to six inches across. The flower heads have yellow centers composed of tubular flowers. These flower heads are of two different types, the female or seed-producing and the male or pollen-producing. The flowers are surrounded by overlapping rows of white bracts that are petal-like and textured like paper. At first glance they are sometimes thought to be the flower petals. It is these bracts that remain after the other flower parts have withered. They last indefinitely in dried flower arrangements—or are everlasting. These long-lasting, pearly white bracts are referred to by the common name. The specific name also means pearly and refers to the white color.

When the flowers are young, the central yellow flowers are not very conspicuous. However, as the flower head matures, the white bracts spread and the center flowers enlarge, becoming more visible. The seeds produced are attached to a tuft of fine, straight hairs that act as a parachute and allow the seeds to spread over great distances.

COMMON CALIFORNIA ASTER   *Aster chilensis*   Composite Family

Common California aster begins blooming in late July or August—and a few blossoms may still be found in January. Occurring in the brushy areas of coastal campgrounds, in damp deflation plains, and in roadside ditches, it is widespread in the western United States. This aster is quite variable. It grows 1 to 3 feet tall and has long, narrow leaves that clasp the stem. The flower heads have yellow or burnt orange disk flowers and narrow purple ray flowers, the entire head being about an inch across.

Asters generally bloom in the late summer or fall and herald the end of summer. Because they bloom when most other coastal wildflowers have been spent, their blossoms stand out and present a spectacular splash of color in openings along roadsides and in woodland borders.

ENGLISH DAISY   *Bellis perennis*   Composite Family

English daisy is a good example of a plant that is not native to the Northwest, yet has adapted quite well and is now common in areas where it does not have to compete with brushy natural vegetation. Most of the leaves are basal, forming a tidy little tuft. The floral head, each on its own stem, has yellow disk flowers and ray flowers that range from white to deep pink. English daisy grows 4 to 6 inches tall but, since it is often found in otherwise neatly manicured lawns, it is sometimes cropped much shorter. Where the lawn is repeatedly mowed, English daisy becomes dwarf, continuing to bloom and dotting the green carpet with white. The flowers may be seen through the winter, spring, and summer months, but are most conspicuous during mild coastal winters when other vegetation is dormant. Look for it in coastal parks and waysides where it often shares the lawns with self-heal and the ubiquitous sea gull.

The Bellis genus is a small one, containing only about a half dozen species. The genus name is derived from the Latin bellis meaning pretty, a reference to the dainty, small flower heads.

COMMON DAISY   *Chrysanthemum leucanthemum*   Composite Family

Everyone knows the common daisy, also known as marguerite and ox-eye daisy. This is the flower daisy chains are made of and the flower renowned by the chant "loves me, loves me not." Growing 12 to 24 inches tall, each of its flower heads is on its own long stem and is about 2 inches across. The disk flowers are yellow while the ray flowers are white. Alternate leaves are scattered along the stem, and are pinnately lobed or parted.

A native of Europe, the common daisy is another example of a plant that reached North American shores with early settlers, either accidentally with seeds mixed in household goods or food items or purposely as garden stock. Common daisy has become widespread and now adorns grassy hillsides and open fields with its gay flowers which bloom through most of the summer.

94

COMMON THISTLE   *Cirsium vulgare*   Composite Family

Thistles are considered weeds by most observers and indeed, they do invade pastures, fields, and areas that are disturbed. They abound in recently logged places as well as roadsides. This is unfortunate because many of the thistle flower heads, close-up, are quite attractive.

Common thistle, also called bull thistle, is a stout plant that grows 2 to 3 feet tall and has spiny irregularly lobed leaves that are decurrent—meaning the base of the leaf has small wings that partially clasp the stem. The purple flower heads are quite conspicuous. A native of Europe, it is now quite widespread in North America and can be found on open grassy coastal headlands and fields.

Many other species of thistle may also be found along the coast; many are difficult to tell apart. Thistles as a group, however, are usually easy to recognize. Their numerous flowers are clustered into a compact head and they usually have prickly stems and leaves. There may be as many as two hundred species of thistle, and many of these are native to North America.

95

SEASIDE DAISY   *Erigeron glaucus*   Composite Family

Seaside daisy inhabits nooks and crannies in basalt cliffs and banks along the Oregon and California coasts. Whether its stems are prostrate or erect, they grow from creeping rhizomes and a stout root, sometimes forming a low-growing mat. The thick leaves are mostly basal, although a few are also scattered along the 2 to 12 inch tall flowering stem. There are from 1 to 6 flowering heads on each stem—the central disk flowers are burnt orange to yellow while the ray flowers range from pink or lavender to almost white. Where the ocean winds and salt spray are severe, the entire plant may be quite dwarf, except for the flower heads which are 1 to 2 inches across. Seaside daisy is never out of sight of the sea and blooms from June through August.

In some areas of the coast, seaside daisy has become a popular garden plant. The tufted form of the plant and the large flowers make it a good garden addition. It can be started either from seed or from cuttings. Seed germinates quickly in sandy soil and can be started either in flats and later transferred or can be sown directly on open ground. During the dry coastal summer, seaside daisy normally thrives on little moisture except for fog. Light watering should assure a long blooming period in the garden.

TANSY RAGWORT   *Senecio jacobaea*   Composite Family

Tansy ragwort, adorned with clusters of yellow flower heads, may be found in open areas along the road, in pastures, and along sand spits and river edges. It covers grassy headlands with a golden hue in July and August. Growing from 1 to 6 feet tall, tansy ragwort has stout stems and leaves that are divided into lobed and toothed segments. The golden-yellow flowering heads are quite numerous, each flower head with 10 to 15 ray flowers surrounding the disk flowers. This makes a clump of them quite conspicuous and colorful, wherever they happen to grow.

A native of Europe, it first became established in the northeastern states, and is now an aggressive weed in the moister portions of Washington, Oregon and California. During the first year, clumps of dark green leaves appear. The following year, the stems grow, branch freely, and produce the colorful flowers for which tansy is known. It has the ability to sprout anew from bits of root that have been cut. Reputed poisonous to livestock, attempts have been made to eradicate it with herbicides and mechanical means. Another promising means of control is the larvae of the cinnabar moth that is highly specialized and feed only on tansy.

CANADA GOLDENROD *Solidago canadensis* Composite Family

Goldenrod flaunts its colorful plumes of flowers during August and September. Widespread in North America, the goldenrod is particularly spectacular along the bluffs overlooking the ocean. Growing from creeping underground stems, a clump of goldenrod resembles a small shrub or bush, and may reach 6 feet in height (although most are 2 to 3 feet tall). The entire stem is leafy, the leaves being lance-shaped and toothed along the edge. The small, yellow flower heads are in thick terminal plumes. Quite common along the coast, this goldenrod grows equally well in fields, meadow edges, and roadsides.

Canada goldenrod could be confused with dune goldenrod, (*Solidago spathulata*), also called sticky goldenrod. It thrives in dune areas that have become partially stabilized. It grows up to 2 feet tall and has spatulate-shaped leaves—as referred to by the species name. Its best diagnostic characteristics however, are the sticky and aromatic leaves that appear to have been recently varnished. This goldenrod colors ocean bluffs and dunes, in late summer and early fall from southern Oregon to central California.

HARVEST BRODIAEA   *Brodiaea coronaria*   Lily Family

Masses of funnel-shaped purple or violet flowers mark this brodiaea. Found on grassy bluffs along the coast from Vancouver Island to California, brodiaeas usually command a magnificent ocean vista. One place to look for them in early summer is the steep slope of Cape Perpetua on the central Oregon coast. You'll find them amid the drying grasses. The cluster of flowers, each on its own short stalk, is on a stem 2 to 10 inches tall, the entire plant somewhat resembling a candelabra.

Blue dicks (*Brodiaea capitata*) is found along the southern Oregon and the California coast. Its deep blue flowers, however, are tightly clustered together, and the plant is much larger, growing between 1 and 2 feet tall.

Both of these brodiaea bloom from late spring through the early part of the summer. Brodiaea bulbs were important in the diet of many coastal Indians. Usually dug with pointed sticks, they were eaten both raw and cooked.

TIGER LILY   *Lilium columbianum*   Lily Family

Also called Columbia lily. Occasionally found on moist hillsides along the coast from British Columbia to northern California, you'll recognize this lily by its nodding flowers with backward curving petals and the whorled leaves. These are mounted along a 1 to 3 foot tall stem. Sometimes specimens 5 to 6 feet tall are found. A great deal of variation occurs in this lily. Flowers may occur singly or a plant may bear many blossoms. The flower color ranges from pale orange to almost yellow to deep burnt orange. Dark purple spots decorate the petals.

Many of the Indians on the Washington coast gathered the bulbs of this lily in quantity, often at the same time they gathered camas bulbs. Usually the bulbs were steamed. Since the bulbs are only about 2 inches in diameter, a great number had to be gathered to make a meal. Therefore, the Indians had to be careful not to deplete their food supply. As with most lilies, one should carefully weigh the need to dig a wild plant. In the case of this lily, its beauty in its natural setting makes it extremely valuable where it is growing.

OREGON IRIS *Iris tenax* Iris Family

Also called purple iris or blue flag. Most people recognize a wild iris because of the cultivated plant. The large, showy flowers have three sepals that turn backward or outward, while the three petals are erect. The cultivated plants have flowers bred for almost any color imaginable; however, the native coastal varieties are usually various shades of blue or purple. Occasionally, cream-colored or yellow specimens occur. They grow along roadsides and on grassy bluffs, either in full sun or partial shade.

Two species grow along the northern Pacific coast. In Oregon and Washington, you'll find *Iris tenax* in open, grassy areas. Usually a single violet or purple (sometimes white) flower is found on each stem, which is 10 to 20 inches tall. Numerous basal leaves and leaf-like bracts along the flowering stem help distinguish this species. The leaves are extremely narrow, almost grasslike, rarely one-fourth inch wide. In open woods along the California coast you are most apt to find *Iris douglasiana*. This iris also has blue or purple flowers. Although its leaves, too, are grasslike, they are usually much wider than those of Oregon iris, being one-fourth to one-half inch wide.

Iris leaves were gathered by coastal Indians for the long, silky fiber found along the margin of each leaf. Scraped clean with a mussel shell, they were twisted and braided. A great amount of work was required to make cord or rope from iris; nonetheless, it was a prime fiber for making fish nets, bags, and small snares.

Brushfields

SILK TASSEL   *Garrya elliptica*   Silk-tassel Family

The silk-tassel is aptly named. Its silvery-colored tassels of flowers gracefully hang from the evergreen shrubs, which grow 3 to 15 feet tall and have wavy-edged leaves. Blooming in the winter or early spring, the pendant flowers become globose fruits only on some of the trees. The male, or pollen-bearing, flowers with their slender, hanging anthers, occur on different plants than the female, or seed-producing, flowers. Only the female shrubs develop fruit. Silk-tassel is fairly common on brushy slopes and hills overlooking the ocean from central Oregon into California.

Another, closely related species, bear brush (*Garrya fremontii*), has smooth-edged leaves. It grows not only along the coast, but also in the Coast Range and inland valleys of southern Oregon and northern California.

103

RED-FLOWERING CURRANT   *Ribes sanguineum*   Saxifrage Family

This brightly-colored shrub is a harbinger of spring. Its blooms, appearing in March and April, signal the end of winter and the beginning of summer. It is one of the earliest of our coastal shrubs to bloom. The pale pink to deep rose-colored flowers are only one-fourth to one-half inch long; however, since they are in pendant clusters about 4 inches long, the mass is quite conspicuous. The leaves are club shaped, with 3 to 5 lobes. Red-flowering currant is a shrub 3 to 12 feet tall. It grows along forest borders and in old logged areas (where it is often found growing on an old stump) as well as on partly re-forested dune areas from British Columbia to central California.

Red-flowering currant could be confused with a closely-related gooseberry, prickly gooseberry (*Ribes menziesii*). It can be found along the coast of California and southern Oregon. It is an upright shrub 3 to 6 feet tall with forked spines along the stem. Smaller bristles occur on the young shoots. The hairy leaves are 1 to 2 inches wide and divided into 3 to 5 lobes. Dark red or purple flowers occur singly or in pairs and these are followed by purple berries, which are covered with fine bristles.

GOAT'S BEARD *Aruncus sylvester* Rose Family

Also called sea foam. A 3 to 6 foot tall plant, goat's beard is best known for its plumes of white flowers. Arranged in narrow pencil-like groups, the flower clusters make a showy display in May and June. Goat's beard is commonly found along shady forest borders. A cosmopolitan plant, it is widespread in North America and also occurs in Eurasia.

The narrow plumes of flowers slowly wither into brownish strings of seed, which persist through part of the winter and aid its identification. At first glance, one would assume this plant is a shrub. However, goat's beard dies back each winter and has no woody tissue, and so is actually an herb. It grows rapidly each spring from an underground stem.

INDIAN PLUM   *Osmaronia cerasiformis*   Rose Family

Also called osoberry, arrowwood. Before any of the coastal brushfields have begun to leaf out, the pendant white flowers of Indian plum begin to bloom. The leaves first appear in small bunches, making them conspicuous against their drab background. Indian plum is a shrub or small tree 4 to 9 feet tall and grows best in the companionship of other shrubby species such as alder and willow. Look for it along roadsides from British Columbia to California.

After the flowers are spent, Indian plum blends into the other greenery. A small berry or "plum" develops by mid-summer. A bluish purple color, it is quite bitter. Although most coastal Indians ate them, they did not regard them as an important part of the diet, probably because of the bitter taste. Robins, cedar waxwings, and other species of birds, however, eat them with relish, often stripping a small shrub of its fruit in only a few hours. Some sources list this shrub as a source of straight wood for arrows.

COMMON WILD ROSE   *Rosa nutkana*   Rose Family

The wild rose is one of the favorites of all wildflowers. Four states (Georgia, Iowa, New York, and North Dakota) have selected a wild rose as their state flower. Usually the wild rose is easily identified as a rose; however, individual species often hybridize and are difficult to tell apart. Wild roses are prickly shrubs with alternate, pinnately compound leaves (meaning the leaflets are arranged along a common shaft, as with a feather). They may be erect, climbing, or trailing along the ground. The flowers usually have five pink petals. The fleshy round fruits are called hips and are rich in vitamin C.

Common wild rose is one of the most conspicuous of our native roses, largely because of its deep pink colored flowers, which may be 2 inches across. It is a stout shrub, armed with stiff prickles and growing 3 to 12 feet tall. It is most often found in moist, wooded areas—look for this wild rose blooming along coastal highways in mid-May and June from Alaska to northern California.

Many coastal Indians used the rose hips for food, some combining them with dried salmon eggs. The peeled twigs and leaves were also boiled and used as a hot beverage. Dried rose hips can be purchased in many health food stores for use in making tea.

HIMALAYAN BLACKBERRY   *Rubus discolor*   Rose Family

Blackberries grow wild on the west side of the Cascade-Sierra chain, brushing over hedgerows, roadside borders, meadows, and other waste areas. They are either a blessing or a bane, depending on whether you desire to pick the berries or attempt to travel through them. There are many species of wild blackberries that can be found along the Pacific coast—Himalayan berry is perhaps the best known, both because of its stout size and its large, tasty berries, which regularly are picked for pies, jam, jelly, and wine. It has large recurved bristles, palmately compound leaves, and thick erect or climbing stems. An introduced species, it is considered a pest by farmers who must eradicate it from their fields. It grows from British Columbia south to California and east to Idaho.

It could be confused with evergreen blackberry (*Rubus laciniatus*), which is also very common. Its leaves, however, are evergreen and the leaflets are deeply lobed. Himalayan blackberry has leaflets that are merely toothed and, although a few leaves may persist through the winter, they are not evergreen.

THIMBLEBERRY   *Rubus parviflorus*   Rose Family

Thimbleberry is a common shrub of the coastal zone. It has large, broadly lobed maple-like leaves whose short hairs give them a velvety texture. A shrub growing 3 to 6 feet high, its stems lack thorns or prickles. The flowers are white, and each of the five petals has a crinkled texture. The red berries which occur at the end of the summer are like soft raspberries and are responsible for the name, thimbleberry. To some, the flavor is rather bland; nonetheless, they make a welcome snack while hiking. Thimbleberry is at home throughout the western states and occurs as far east as the Great Lakes area.

SALMONBERRY *Rubus spectabilis* Rose Family

Salmonberry is quite common along roadsides and brushfields throughout the moist climate area of the Pacific Northwest. It is a shrub growing 3 to 12 feet tall and is responsible for the dense shrubby growth along much of U.S. 101. Its tangled mass impedes hikers and cross-country travelers. It has leaves divided into three coursely-toothed leaflets, small thorns on its stems, and five-petaled rose-red flowers that are about an inch wide. These bloom in April and May, sometimes hanging partially hidden beneath the overhanging leaves. Often, scattered blossoms will be found throughout the summer months. The berries, which somewhat resemble raspberries, come in two colors: a clear orange and a deeper red. Both provide good munching but the clear orange berry is usually considered the most tasty.

110

SCOTCH BROOM   *Cytisus scoparius*   Pea Family

This gaily-flowered shrub is extremely conspicuous along the coast, especially when it is at the peak of its flowering in May. The golden flowers color dry slopes, road shoulders, bluffs, and dune areas, where it has been planted in the past for sand stabilization. Although most flowers are pure yellow, occasionally they are spotted with purple or maroon. This shrub grows up to 9 feet tall and has small, three-parted leaves and angled, green stems. The brightly colored flowers are replaced by dark, hairy pods, which pop open when ripe, scattering seeds in every direction. On a warm still day, you can hear the crackling, popping sound.

A similar-appearing shrub is becoming common along the coast at various locations. This is French broom (*Cytisus monspessulanus*). Its flowers are a pale yellow and are in small clusters of 3 to 10. Those of Scotch broom are usually solitary, occurring in the axils of the leaves.

Neither of these shrubs is native to our coast. Scotch broom is believed to have been introduced near Victoria, British Columbia, in the 1850's when seeds from the British consul in the Sandwich Islands, as Hawaii was then called, were planted. Although only a few of the plants grew, it was enough to establish this aggressive shrub in the Northwest coast. French broom, likewise, is not a native plant. Scotch broom is originally from Europe; French broom is a native of the Canary Islands and is now found along the coast from southern California to Washington. It, too, was introduced as a garden plant.

111

FIREWEED   *Epilobium angustifolium*   Evening Primrose Family

Fireweed colors abandoned fields, cut-over forest areas, and burned areas—fireweed's habit of growing in this latter area accounts for the common name. Another common name is willow-herb, because of the resemblance of the leaves to those of the willow.

Fireweed grows up to 7 feet tall, with spear-shaped leaves along the entire length. The plume of pink or red flowers, however, is fireweed's most distinctive feature. They begin to bloom in early summer, the flower cluster blooming from the bottom upward. The flowers are followed by thin seed pods or capsules that split linearly into four parts when ripe. The seeds are expelled. Each carries a feathery plume that aids its dispersion. Fireweed spreads not only by seeds but also by buds on the underground stems.

Fireweed has long been used in northern areas for food—the young shoots are cut and eaten like asparagus. It is also well-known for its nectar. Bee-keepers regularly seek out prime fireweed areas for the production of honey. Few coastal Indians, however, are known to have used fireweed as a food supply. Perhaps, because of the lack of openings in the dense timber, there were not enough sunny, brushy spots to encourage fireweed growth.

MADRONE   *Arbutus menziesii*   Heath Family

This evergreen, broad-leaved tree is one of the most beautiful to be found anywhere on the Pacific Coast. It occurs from British Columbia to Baja, California. Greatly resembling an overgrown manzanita to which it is closely related, madrone or Pacific madrone grows up to 90 feet tall, has shiny red bark, pendant clusters of white, urn-shaped flowers, and bright scarlet berries. They bloom along Highway 101 in April and May, making a spectacular spring display.

Madrone had many uses among both the Indians and the early settlers. The root, bark, and leaves were steeped in water to make a brew for colds. The bark, which rolls off each year, was used to make a tea for soothing stomachaches. The hard wood was used as support for Indian dwellings and for the making of many small tools, such as digging sticks.

The first botanical explorer to note the madrone was Archibald Menzies, who sailed to the Pacific Coast with the Vancouver Expedition of 1790. This intrepid traveler was the first white man to see many of the Northwest's most famous and conspicuous plants, including the Douglas fir and the redwood.

SALAL   *Gaultheria shallon*   Heath Family

Salal is well-known to most residents of the Pacific Northwest. It can be barely 6 inches tall or a robust bush of 5 feet or more. It attains its most luxuriant growth along the forest borders and brushfields of the Pacific Coast where the wind often prunes it into a thick, impenetrable hedge. The evergreen leaves are thick and leathery, 3 to 4 inches long. Urn-shaped flowers bloom from May through July and are followed by juicy blue-black berries.

Coastal Indians used the salal berries in a variety of ways. Usually they were mashed so that they could be dried in small cakes. Later these cakes were dipped in whale oil or seal oil and eaten. They were also eaten fresh but, again, with oil from a whale or seal. Sometimes the salal was dried in large quantities and shaped into large loaves resembling bread. Early settlers learned to make a syrup and pies from the salal berry; it also makes an excellent jam or jelly.

Salal was one of David Douglas' favorite North American plants. (David Douglas was an early Northwest botanist who collected extensively in 1825-1826 along the Columbia River drainage while staying at Ft. Vancouver, a Hudson's Bay Company post.) He introduced it into Europe, where it has been used as a garden planting. Only recently has it come into its own for landscaping in the Northwest. Its large, evergreen leaves make an excellent ground cover.

PACIFIC RHODODENDRON   *Rhododendron macrophyllum*   Heath Family

A visit to the Pacific Coast in May or June is a color treat. The brilliant gold of scotch broom blends with the deep purple or rose-red of the Pacific rhododendron. An evergreen shrub five to ten feet tall, it attains a neat, compact form when in the open but more often is a straggling, sparsely branched shrub when it is part of the forest understory. The blossoms form clusters six inches or more across and are especially spectacular against the green background of the forest edge. The leathery, oblong leaves have slightly rolled-under edges.

The name rhododendron comes from the Greek for rose tree, attesting to the renowned beauty of the genus in ancient times. Today, the Pacific rhododendron is widely acclaimed as one of the most beautiful of our native shrubs. It has been declared the state flower of Washington and several coastal communities have festivals to commemorate the time of blooming. Many horticultural varieties have been developed and grace lawns and gardens. Although the native rhododendron is generally a pale pink or rose color, commercial nurseries now offer shrubs with flowers ranging from white and yellow to deep purple.

119

WESTERN AZALEA   *Rhododendron occidentale*   Heath Family

A spectacular shrub of coastal brushfields when it blooms in late April and May, azalea often forms dense thickets. The clusters of fragrant, funnel-shaped flowers adorn 2 to 14 foot tall shrubs that are often pruned and battered by coastal winds. The 1 to 2 inch long flowers are pink or white, and have a large yellow blotch on the inner part of the upper lobe. The five stamens extend beyond the flower tube, adding to the beauty of the flower.

Where the azalea occurs along the coast, many local communities celebrate "azalea days" to herald the coming of summer. It occurs from the southern Oregon to central California coast and in the Sierra Nevada of California.

When found inland, the western azalea may become a spreading and graceful shrub. In this form, it has found its way into many Northwestern gardens and parks, where it does best in well-watered, partially shaded sites. Like its close relatives the Pacific rhododendron and salal, it prefers acid soil. Gardeners have their best success in growing native plants when they closely observe the natural growing conditions and re-create them as closely as they possibly can.

EVERGREEN HUCKLEBERRY   *Vaccinium ovatum*   Heath Family

An evergreen shrub found in shaded areas of the coast from British Columbia to northern California, this huckleberry has shiny, leathery oblong or ovate leaves with toothed edges. The bell-shaped flowers are pale pink and are in small clusters hanging from the axils of the leaves. The tasty black berries that appear at the end of the summer are readily gathered by coastal residents and travelers alike. You'll find campers along the coast who regularly visit their favorite campground to pick ripe huckleberries. These tasty fruits are then made into jams, jellies, pies and syrups. This huckleberry also makes a good landscaping plant. The shiny leaves are evergreen, which makes it attractive year around.

A huckleberry that is found in dense woodlands, in partial shade or even in open areas, red huckleberry (*Vaccinium parvifolium*) is characterized by urn-shaped flowers, thin pale green leaves, bright red berries, and stems that are distinctly angled. The berries are much sparser in this species and therefore more difficult to gather. This huckleberry is often seen growing from the stumps remaining in areas that have been cut over or burned. These plants were probably planted by birds using the stumps as perches or resting posts. Red huckleberry is found in lowland forests from British Columbia to central California.

RED ELDERBERRY   *Sambucus racemosa*   Honeysuckle Family

Red elderberry grows in moist forest edges and sunny coastal campgrounds from southern Alaska to central California. A small tree or shrub growing 5 to 20 feet tall, red elderberry is recognized in the spring and early summer by its pyramidal cluster of white flowers and compound leaves of five leaflets. Red elderberry acquires its common name, however, from its bright red fruit. The clusters of red berries attract as much attention as the plumes of flowers making it an attractive shrub in coastal areas nearly all summer. These berries are eaten by a wide variety of animals. Flocks of band-tailed pigeons, for instance, feast on them, often completely consuming the crop.

The red elderberry could possibly be confused with the blue elderberry (*Sambucus cerulea*). It is often found in coastal valleys. The flower cluster is flat, not dome-shaped, as in the red elderberry. The fruits are a pale blue.

CHAPPARRAL BROOM *Baccharis pilularis* Composite Family

Found on bluffs and banks along the Oregon and California coasts, chapparral broom also known as coyote bush, blooms in the fall. It is a much branched shrub growing 2 to 5 feet tall, with alternate, irregularly toothed, leathery leaves, and flowers in small clusters. Like the flowers of the silk tassel the seed-bearing flowers are on different plants than the pollen-bearing flowers. By January or February the female flowers have become silky puffs of seed heads that fill the air. Because it blooms when most other plants have become dormant, chapparral broom is quite conspicuous. It is also noticeable because its leaves are evergreen, making them stand out against the subdued browns and golds of autumn.

Coastal Forest

WILD GINGER   *Asarum caudatum*   Birthwort Family

Growing freely through the leaf mold of damp coastal woodlands, the heart-shaped leaves of wild ginger are easily recognized both by their shape and their velvety-textured surface. The dark rose-colored flowers are hidden beneath the leaves and hug the ground. The flowers are cup-shaped with three lobes, each of which has a long, tapering tip. The sprawling wild ginger rarely grows more than a few inches tall and blooms during the spring and early summer along the coast from British Columbia to northern California.

The scaly rootstocks of *Asarum* are quite fragrant, emitting the scent of ginger. While these rootstocks have been used as a seasoning in natural food recipes, they are too mild to be used commercially.

CANDYFLOWER   *Montia sibirica*   Purslane Family

Although the individual flowers are small, candyflower often sprawls over the ground in dense shade, dotting the forest floor with its white flowers. Look carefully at these five-petaled flowers—each petal has a notch in the tip. Most of the leaves are basal, meaning they emerge from the base of the plant on their own stems. The 5 to 12 inch flowering stem however, also has two leaves. These are sessile, meaning they have no petiole, but are attached directly to the flowering stem and do not have a stalk of their own. Also known as western spring beauty, these little plants are widespread in the western states where they have long been used as salad greens.

MINER'S LETTUCE *Montia perfoliata* Purslane Family

Miner's lettuce sprawls across the forest duff in dry woodlands or hugs the ground in a tight rosette of basal leaves in sandy openings, especially in dune areas that are partially vegetated or moist in the spring. It inhabits a variety of places from the coast and valley bottoms to forested mountains. It occurs throughout most of the western states. Miner's lettuce is distinguished from the closely related candyflower by the two leaves on the floral stem, which completely enclose it, while those of candyflower are separate.

The name miner's lettuce comes from the plant's edible leaves. It is common in the mountain foothills frequented by pioneer prospectors. These miners probably learned of the plant from native Americans. Early accounts relate how Indians gathered the plant or simply ate it in place. The succulent leaves can be eaten either cooked or raw, like any other green. Mixed with other raw vegetables, it makes an excellent salad.

127

WILD BLEEDINGHEART   *Dicentra formosa*   Fumitory Family

Bleedingheart flowers are uniquely heart-shaped baskets composed of four pale purple or pink petals. Slightly less than an inch long, they hang from 10 to 20 inch tall stems. Bleedingheart leaves rise from stout rootstocks and are finely divided, somewhat resembling a fern leaf. You'll find these flowers in full bloom in the springtime and the early part of the summer, although you may still find a few blossoms in sheltered places in July or August. Bleedingheart grows best in moist, shady woodlands. You'll find it amid the moss of redwoods, Douglas fir, spruce, and hemlock from western British Columbia to western California.

CORYDALIS   *Corydalis scouleri*   Fumitory Family

Corydalis is closely related to bleedingheart. Its flowers, however, are not neatly symmetrical sacks; instead of both outer petals being sack-like to make a heart-shaped flower, only one of the outer petals is spurred or sack-shaped. The resulting flower is a long, tubular affair, about one-half inch long. The spur is twice as long as the rest of the petal. The rose-colored flowers are clustered at the end of a 10 to 20 inch tall, leafy stem. The seeds are encased in a fat, cylindric capsule that explodes at the slightest touch, catapulting the seeds a considerable distance. This wildflower occurs in moist woodlands from British Columbia to Oregon.

129

FRINGECUPS   *Tellima grandiflora*   Saxifrage Family

Fringecups is well-named. Each flower is a small, cup-shaped affair with fringed edges, which turn backward. Arranged linearly along a stem from 1 to 3 feet tall, they vary in color from pink or red to pale green or white. Most of the leaves are basal. Fringecups can be found growing in shaded spots among the mossy rocks and boulders which form most of the high basalt cliffs of the coast. They bloom in April, May and June. They also grow inland, but they are usually found in moist, shaded woodlands and occur from southern Alaska to central California.

130

YOUTH-ON-AGE   *Tolmiea menziesii*   Saxifrage Family

Also called pig-a-back plant and thousand mothers. The most interesting characteristic of this plant does not occur until late summer or fall. The 1 to 3 inch wide leaves are heart-shaped, with irregularly lobed margins. The plant can reproduce small buds at the base of these leaves, thus giving rise to most of its common names. Each leaf appears to carry another, smaller leaf "piggy-back." Many people collect youth-on-age to use for a house plant because of its rich, leafy growth. The flowers, which are maroon or even rust colored, occur on a linear stem 1 to 2 feet long and bloom in May and June. This delightful little plant grows in shaded areas and forest edges from Alaska south to California.

The scientific name honors two great men of the early Northwest. Dr. William F. Tolmie was a surgeon at Ft. Vancouver for the Hudson's Bay Company during the mid-1800's. Archibald Menzies was a naturalist with the Vancouver Expedition of 1790 to 1795 that explored the Pacific Coast. His early observations added a great deal to the early knowledge about the Northwest.

131

WOOD SORREL   *Oxalis oregana*   Wood Sorrel Family

The dainty clover-shaped leaves of this ground-hugging plant often cover much of the forest floor at lower elevations from the Olympic Peninsula to California. They fold together at night and on cloudy days and droop when exposed to strong sunlight. Their mass effect creates a conspicuous carpet that is often more noticeable than the flowers which are tucked down between the leaves. There is quite a bit of variation in the color of the flowers. Under the redwoods they often exhibit a deep pink color, while along the northern coast they are usually white. There may also be differences in the leaves; some display distinctive white markings, while others are an even green.

The name oxalis refers to the oxalic acid found in the plant. This gives the leaves a rather tart taste. The leaves are edible and add a pleasing tang to green salads. Wood sorrel is sometimes introduced into shaded gardens as a ground cover. A fairly aggressive plant, it spreads rapidly by underground stems. These allow it to quickly fill in a shady nook, often to the exclusion of other plants. Its attractive foliage has also earned its way indoors as a house plant.

132

WOOD VIOLET   *Viola glabella*   Violet Family

Most of us think of violets as purple flowers. However, most of the Northwest's native violets are yellow or a combination of white, blue, or yellow. This yellow-flowered violet has erect, leafy stems 6 to 12 inches tall and broad, heart-shaped leaves. They spread from a horizontal rootstock, a trait which makes it a good ground cover for native gardens. The irregular five-petaled flower has the characteristic shape of other members of this group. There are two lateral petals, two upper petals, and one lower petal that is spurred at the base. In wood violet, the lateral and lower petals are dark-veined. This violet grows in moist woodlands from Alaska to California.

Wood violet could be confused with evergreen violet, also called redwoods violet (*Viola sempervirens*), which is also common in coastal woodlands, particularly in the deep duff of redwood forests. This yellow-flowered violet has prostrate stems and round, evergreen leaves. The lower and lateral petals of the flower are marked with purple.

The Viola genus has an interesting back-up mechanism for producing seeds. The large showy flowers are often not fertile and do not produce an abundant supply of seeds. Later in the season, small flowers are produced near the ground. These do not open and are self-fertilized. Thus, a supplemental seed source helps insure the continuance of the species.

133

SPRING QUEEN   *Synthyris reniformis*   Figwort Family

Also called grouse flower. One of our earliest blooming wildflowers, spring queen begins unfolding its dainty blue flowers in mid-February. Although occasionally found on partially sunny banks, it is most often found on a mossy bed in shaded areas throughout western Oregon and western Washington. It grows 2 to 8 inches tall, with basal leaves that are kidney to heart-shaped. These partially cover the delicate flowers, which are borne in small clusters of six to eight. Look closely at the individual flowers. Two purple-tipped stamens protrude from the basket which is formed by four pale purple or blue petals. Because of Spring queen's small size, it is often necessary to get down on hands and knees and part the fallen leaves and clumps of moss under which it grows to see these delightful little flowers.

The name spring queen comes from the early blooming date of the flowers. Although a lowly plant in stature, its early arrival during the spring makes it the queen of the forest. The name grouse flower comes from its association with the mating time of the sooty or blue grouse. The soft hooting sounds of the grouse may be heard in the woods at the same time this flower is blooming.

GROUND CONE   *Boschniakia hookeri*   Broom-rape Family

It takes a sharp eye to spot ground cone. Resembling a stout, over-sized fir-cone squatting on the forest floor, ground cone is well-named. The fleshy stems are 3 to 6 inches tall and the entire plant is purple or, sometimes, pale yellow. The leaves are merely overlapping bracts that partially conceal the flowers, which are sessile and attach directly to the stout little stem.

Ground cone is a fairly host specific parasitic plant, deriving its nourishment from the roots of chlorophyll-bearing (green) plants and is most often associated with salal. You'll find ground cone in May and June in the sandy soil of dunes that have become covered with a coastal forest of spruce, huckleberry, and salal from Vancouver Island to central California.

In southern Oregon and California another ground cone is found—*Boschniakia strobilacea*. Its bracts are widest at their upper end while those of *Boschniakia hookeri* are widest across the middle.

COLTSFOOT *Petasites frigidus* Composite Family

Competing with skunk cabbage for the title of "earliest blooming wildflower" coltsfoot begins to emerge from the soil in mid-February and March. First, a miniature parasol-like leaf unfolds, then the button-like flower stalk appears. When it first begins to bloom, the flowering stalk is merely a few inches tall; however, after a few weeks it grows to about 12 inches. The round cluster of flowers is at the tip of a thick stem that has scale-like leaves along its length. The tubular florets of the flower head are pale pink or lavender, sometimes white. As they wither, the parasol-like leaf expands and remains for the rest of the summer. These leaves have soft, woolly hairs on their undersides and grow nearly a foot across. Coltsfoot may be found in the leaf duff of lowland forests and along shady, moist roadbanks. Occurring across northern North America and Eurasia, coltsfoot extends south in the Pacific states to central California.

136

WOOD TRILLIUM   *Trillium ovatum*   Lily Family

Wood trillium is one of the Northwest's favorite wildflowers. Beginning to bloom in late March, when the rest of the forest floor is still clothed in winter brown, the large white blossoms stand out against the subdued background. Growing from 6 to 24 inches tall, each trillium bears three whorled leaves near the upper portion of the stem. These cradle the three-petaled flower, which has its own short stalk. As the flower matures, its pure white color turns pale pink and, finally, deep rose. You'll find this trillium in shady spots throughout the Northwest, from British Columbia to central California and east to Colorado and Wyoming.

Trilliums are among the most familiar of North American wildflowers. Because they bloom so early, they often become favorite components of springtime bouquets.

A word of caution might be made here. A great amount of the stored food stuff from the previous year is expended to produce the flowering stem. The trillium has only three leaves with which to manufacture new food for growth. The picking of the flowering stem usually results in the death of the entire plant. Without the green leaves and stem, the plant cannot survive. So . . . leave the flowers in the field to enjoy next year.

137

SESSILE TRILLIUM   *Trillium chloropetalum*   Lily Family

Sessile trillium is easily distinguished from the wood trillium because its flower is nestled against the three leaves. Lacking a stalk of its own, the flower is "sessile." This species has a great deal of variety: the flowers vary from pale yellow or green to pink or red; the leaves are often mottled with dark patterns. Sessile trillium occurs in the shady woodlands of western Washington, Oregon, and northern California.

138

FALSE-LILY-OF-THE-VALLEY   *Maianthemum dilatatum*   Lily Family

Also known as may-lily, deerberry, beadruby. Carpets of this little lily cover the ground beneath the dense shade of coastal forests from Alaska to northern California. The plant spreads easily by underground stems, allowing it to cover large areas. The shiny green heart-shaped leaves are attractive all summer long. They emerge in the early spring, rolled into an oblong sheath as they emerge from the soil. In May and June the 12-inch tall stems of white flowers appear. These are tightly clustered at the upper portion of the stem, creating a linear tassel of white. Red berries appear in late summer.

FALSE SOLOMON'S SEAL   *Smilacina racemosa*   Lily Family

A plume of small white flowers at the end of an unbranched stem distinguishes false Solomon's seal. Growing from 1 to 3 feet tall from a creeping underground stem, false Solomon's seal is common in shaded conifer forests. The flowers bloom from April through June along the Pacific Coast. By the end of the summer they are replaced by red berries.

False Solomon's seal could be confused with the closely related star-flowered Solomon's seal (*Smilicina stellata*). However, it is much smaller, growing 12 to 24 inches tall.

CALYPSO   *Calypso bulbosa*   Orchid Family

This delicate member of the large Orchid Family is one of the most beautiful of our native wildflowers. That it is endeared by many may be attested to by the large number of common names which have been fondly bestowed upon it: fairy slipper, deer-head orchid, Venus slipper, slipper orchid, angel slipper, redwoods orchid. The distinctive slipper-shaped flower rides atop a short (six inch) stalk, which has a sheathing, scale-like round leaf at its base. The flower is a reddish-purple color and appears in May. After the flower withers, the single leaf also wilts making the entire plant nearly undetectable during most of the summer. In the fall a new leaf emerges from the small corm which is the underground bulb-like swelling at the base of the stem. This leaf then persists throughout the winter months.

The name Calypso is derived from the Greek meaning hidden or covered from view. Indeed, this little plant is well-named for it thrives only when growing in the deep duff of moist woodlands where its diminuative size makes it easy to overlook. The Calypso is a widespread species, occurring over much of western and northern North America and also in Eurasia.

Index